EQUALITY OF NATIONS

EQUALITY OF NATIONS

FOSTERING FAIRNESS, EQUITY, JUSTICE AND CO-OPERATION AMONG NATIONS

Dr. Dominion V. Judah

Equality of Nations
Dr. Dominion V. Judah

First Edition, 2023

Publisher's Name: The Ageless Press

ISBN: Hardback Edition: 978-0-6458613-2-7
ISBN: Paperback Edition 978-0-6458613-3-4
ISBN: Ebook Edition 978-0-6458613-4-1

TABLE OF CONTENTS

INTRODUCTION 1

CHAPTER ONE 3

THE SOVEREIGNTY OF NATIONS AND EXTERNAL CONTROLS..........8

The Shifting Dynamics of Sovereignty in a Globalized World

Balancing Sovereignty with the Necessity of International Cooperation

The Impacts of External Influences on National Sovereignty

The Complex Landscape of Interdependence

CHAPTER TWO 32

THE NEED FOR BETTER ECONOMIC GLOBAL ARCHITECTURE

Current Flaws in the Global Economic System

Pursuing Economic Architecture that Fosters Equality and Inclusion

Role of International Institutions in Shaping Equitable Economic Policies

Crafting a Blueprint for Global Economic Reform

CHAPTER THREE 55

ECONOMIC EQUALITY THROUGH INCLUSIVE MULTILATERAL ARCHITECTURES

Treating Nations as Equals

Empowering Local Currencies and Settlements

Responsible Resource Management

Inclusivity of Reserve Currencies

Sustainable Growth and Development

CHAPTER FOUR 81
EQUAL RIGHTS OF NATIONS
The Fundamental Principle of Equal Rights Among Nations
Historical and Current Examples of Inequality Among Nations
Overcoming Hurdles to Implementing Equal Rights Globally
Securing Equal Rights for All Nations: A Journey of Collaborative Love and Respect

CHAPTER FIVE 105
SOVEREIGNTY AND COOPERATION
The Interplay Between Sovereignty and Effective Global Cooperation
Navigating Challenges in Balancing National Autonomy and Global Unity
Collaborative Diplomacy
Forging a New Paradigm

CHAPTER SIX 124
MULTILATERAL AGREEMENTS AND EQUALITY OF VOTES
The Evolution and Efficacy of Multilateral Agreements
Evaluating the Role of Voting Equality in Global Decision-Making
Addressing Impediments to Equal Voting Representation

CHAPTER SEVEN 143
ENVIRONMENTAL JUSTICE AND GLOBAL RESPONSIBILITY
The Environmental Impacts of Global Disparities
Creating a Level-Playing Field for Environmental Responsibility
The Role of International Agreements in Environmental Equity
Sustainability and Collaboration: Charting a Sustainable Future

CHAPTER EIGHT 163
CULTURAL EXCHANGE AND MUTUAL UNDERSTANDING
Embracing Diversity and Fostering Mutual Understanding
Cultural Diplomacy: A Catalyst for Harmonious International Relations
Global Citizenship: The Power of Shared Cultural Experiences
Promoting Cultural Exchange for Enhanced Global Solidarity

CHAPTER NINE 182

ENSURING JUSTICE AND ACCOUNTABILITY
Upholding Accountability in International Relations
Addressing Injustices Through International Legal Frameworks
Truth and Reconciliation: Navigating the Path to Global Justice
Creating a World Where Justice Prevails for All Nations

CONCLUSION 208

REFERENCES.. 211

INTRODUCTION

Equality of nations is a profound principle that encapsulates the essence of fair treatment, mutual respect, and balanced interactions between all sovereign states across the globe. It is rooted in the belief that every nation, regardless of its size, history, or socio-economic status, deserves an equal voice, opportunity, and recognition on the international stage. This concept goes beyond the mere absence of discrimination or bias; it aspires to create a world where nations cooperate, coexist, and thrive in a collaborative ecosystem that nurtures global equity and solidarity.

In a dynamic and interconnected world, the concept of equality among nations takes center stage as an essential cornerstone of international relations. This principle underscores the crucial endeavor to foster a harmonious and sustainable global society where nations come together to address shared challenges, harness collective strengths, and celebrate the rich tapestry of human diversity. Beyond its theoretical implications, the equality of nations is a pragmatic approach that acknowledges the interdependence of our planet's inhabitants and seeks to ensure that no nation is left behind in the pursuit of progress.

The essence of equality among nations lies in its ability to transcend borders, ideologies, and historical narratives. It is recognition that each nation possesses intrinsic value and potential regardless of its past or present circumstances. This principle engenders a mindset of inclusivity and empathy, fostering an environment where nations cooperate not out of compulsion but out of a genuine desire to uplift one another and contribute to the greater common good.

At its core, the quest for global equity and collaborative harmony represents a departure from the traditional power dynamics that have often characterized international relations. It envisions a world where influence is wielded not as a tool of dominance but as a means to facilitate cooperation, resolve conflicts, and advance shared objectives. This transformative vision challenges nations to reevaluate their roles and responsibilities on the global stage, encouraging them to contribute actively to the well-being of their citizens and the broader global community.

The significance of equality among nations extends beyond diplomatic rhetoric; it permeates diverse aspects of human existence. Economically, it underscores the importance of fostering a level playing field where nations can engage in trade, investment, and technological innovation without undue barriers. Politically, it promotes diplomacy over confrontation, encouraging dialogue and negotiation as the preferred methods for resolving disputes. Furthermore, it enhances the unified stance of nations in tackling urgent global concerns, including climate change, public health emergencies, and humanitarian crises.

This book delves deeper into the multifaceted dimensions of equality among nations. We examine its historical underpinnings, analyze its implications for contemporary international relations, and illuminate its transformative potential for shaping a more just and interconnected world. Through a comprehensive lens, we will uncover the stories, initiatives, and individuals who have championed the cause of global equity and collaborative harmony, paving the way for a future where nations stand shoulder to shoulder, united by the shared aspiration for a better world.

CHAPTER ONE

THE SOVEREIGNTY OF NATIONS AND EXTERNAL CONTROLS

In international relations, national sovereignty is a bedrock principle, signifying a state's independent authority over its internal affairs within defined borders. It encapsulates a nation's autonomy, right to self-governance, and capacity to make decisions aligned with its interests and values.

However, the landscape of the modern world is far from confined by geographical boundaries. Globalization, technological advancement, and the interdependence of nations have woven a complex web of interactions that challenge the traditional understanding of sovereignty. External controls arising from international agreements, alliances, and supranational organizations, exert influence beyond national borders.

This chapter explains the intricate interplay between the sovereignty of nations and the forces of external controls. It navigates the nuanced tension that emerges as states strive to assert their autonomy while engaging in an increasingly interconnected global arena. The juxtaposition of sovereignty and external controls paints a dynamic picture, highlighting both the opportunities and challenges that arise from international collaboration.

Historically, sovereignty emerged as a response to the upheaval of conflicts, solidifying the concept of nation-states as distinct, autonomous entities. Over time, the world has witnessed the evolution of international norms and agreements that bind nations together to pursue common objectives. These external controls, from trade pacts to environmental accords, reflect the collective recognition that some challenges transcend national borders and necessitate cooperative action.

Yet, the interaction between sovereignty and external controls is complex. Striking a delicate balance requires careful consideration of a nation's unique circumstances, strategic interests, and the evolving global landscape. The push and pull between asserting self-governance and participating in collaborative endeavors define the diplomatic intricacies of our time.

As the global stage evolves, questions arise regarding how external controls should influence a nation's decision-making processes.

The growth of global challenges like climate change and transnational terrorism has highlighted the necessity for coordinated solutions that go beyond individual state acts. This poses a basic question: How can countries work together to solve problems without losing their sovereignty?

This chapter embarks on a journey to explore the intricate interplay between the sovereignty of nations and the forces of external controls. Through historical insights and comprehensive analysis of international relations, we will unravel the threads that weave together these seemingly opposing forces. We will delve into the nuances of diplomatic negotiations, the dynamics of power, and the evolving norms that shape the relationship between nations and the broader global community.

THE SHIFTING DYNAMICS OF SOVEREIGNTY IN A GLOBALIZED WORLD

Since its emergence in the seventeenth century, the concept of sovereign states has wielded an indelible influence over the landscape of political governance and economic interactions. Rooted in historical legacies and nurtured by the evolution of human societies, this concept has assumed unparalleled significance, serving as the cornerstone upon which the edifices of modern nations have been erected. Sovereignty, once a monolithic symbol of a nation's self-governing authority, has embarked on a transformative journey, expanding its boundaries to encompass intricate layers of meaning and traversing the intricate tapestry of national and international dimensions. This profound metamorphosis, catalyzed by globalization's inexorable march and propelled by non-state actors' ascent onto the global stage, has ushered in an era of reimagined sovereignty, challenging entrenched paradigms and reshaping the essence of statehood.

Sovereignty's National Anchorage and International Constitutionalization

The emergence of sovereignty marked a pivotal juncture in the annals of political philosophy, fundamentally altering the landscape of governance and statehood. Rooted in the seventeenth century, sovereignty's inception heralded a transformative epoch wherein nation-states were vested with unparalleled authority over their internal affairs. This national sovereignty, a cornerstone of governance, found its apotheosis in the sanctum of the national constitution. This instrument enshrined the collective will of a people and signaled their resolute quest for self-determination.

As the embodiment of a populace's aspirations, the national constitution served as a formal testament to the birth of a distinct mode of self-rule. It encapsulated the ethos of a society's values, ideals, and governance principles, laying the foundation for a governance structure that echoed the voices of the governed. This legal construct was a potent expression of sovereignty's "final authority," a proclamation that within the hallowed bounds of a nation's territorial sovereignty, the constitution's imprints held sway over all matters, from lawmaking to policy formulation.

Simultaneously, the international stage bore witness to sovereignty's transcendent evolution. While predominantly concerned with regulating interstate relations, international law became an arbiter of sovereign equality. The principle of equal sovereign rights resonated through the corridors of global diplomacy, underpinning the autonomy of state law and fostering an international environment where the authority of sovereign states remained unassailable. This duality – the national constitution as the epicenter of self-governance and international law as the custodian of sovereign equality – constituted a symphonic harmony, each note reinforcing the legitimacy of the other.

The interplay between these realms introduced a nuanced symmetry, revealing the interwoven fabric of national and international sovereignty. The national constitution, an articulation of self-determination, resonated within the international legal framework, testifying to a state's constitutional identity and reinforcing its autonomy on the global stage. This reciprocity between the national and international dimensions not only safeguarded the primacy of national governance but also highlighted the intricate tapestry of sovereignty's multifaceted manifestation.

In essence, sovereignty's dual nature served as a unifying force that bridged the chasm between domestic and international spheres. While a testament to the aspirations of a sovereign people, the national constitution reverberated beyond borders, echoing within the chambers of international diplomacy. International law equally recognized the sanctity of statehood, ensuring that the autonomy enshrined in national constitutions remained undiminished within the realm of global interactions.

As the narrative of sovereignty continues to unfold in our contemporary global landscape, this intricate duality remains a beacon of exploration. The national constitutions, steeped in the ethos of self-governance and international law, guided by principles of equality, forge an inseparable alliance that navigates the ever-shifting currents of statehood. In this dynamic interplay, sovereignty's voyage straddles the national and the international, encapsulating the essence of self-determination while harmonizing with the imperatives of global cooperation.

Erosion of Traditional Sovereignty

The seismic ripples of globalization have etched an indelible mark on the bedrock of sovereignty, prompting a profound reevaluation of its traditional moorings. The once-firm contours of sovereign authority have undergone a metamorphic transformation, yielding to the inexorable forces of a borderless world. In this intricate dance, non-state actors – the intergovernmental organizations (IGOs), international nongovernmental organizations (INGOs), and transnational corporations (TNCs) – have emerged as potent players, assuming roles of extraordinary significance within the theater of global affairs.

Gone are the days when these non-state entities languished on the periphery as passive observers. Instead, they have risen as formidable participants, wielding influence far beyond national boundaries. Their narratives intertwine with those of sovereign states, shaping policies, driving agendas, and championing causes that transcend the confines of individual nations. This symphony of global dynamics, composed by the interplay of states and non-state actors, weaves a tapestry that is at once intricate and transformative.

This symbiotic relationship between sovereign states and non-state actors catalyzes transnationalization, blurring the lines between state law and international law. The traditional demarcations delineating the sphere of sovereign control have begun to fade as international norms intermingle with domestic policies, culminating in a "progressive" fusion. This fusion manifests the evolving role of non-state actors in shaping the contours of international legal paradigms, leading to a recalibration of the traditional understanding of sovereignty itself.

In this era of interconnectedness, sovereignty no longer adheres to the narrow confines of national borders. It transcends geographic limitations and extends its reach into collaborative global governance. The once-sacrosanct notion that sovereignty thrives in isolation has given way to a new reality, where its essence is interwoven with the influence of non-state actors, the imperatives of international cooperation, and the shared pursuit of common goals.

This erosion of traditional sovereignty, far from heralding a diminution of state power, ushers in an era of unprecedented possibilities. The symphony of global dynamics, with its harmonious interplay between sovereign states and non-state actors, underscores the necessity of a new paradigm that embraces the complexities of a globalized world while upholding the core tenets of self-governance. As sovereignty navigates this intricate dance, it redefines its role, not as an insular fortress but as a dynamic force that thrives on collaboration, adapts to transnational challenges, and envisions a future where the collective destinies of nations and non-state actors are intertwined in a shared symphony of global progress.

Proliferation of Specialized Regimes

The unfolding narrative of sovereignty encounters a new chapter with the proliferation of specialized international law regimes, heralding an era where the threads of its traditional tapestry begin to unravel even further. These regimes, characterized by their intricate interplay between national autonomy and global collaboration, delve into the heart of major domestic policy domains, transcending the confines of the traditional Westphalian model that once epitomized state-centric orientations.

As these transnational regulatory frameworks gain prominence, the dynamics of sovereignty experience a profound reconfiguration. No longer is the state the exclusive arbiter of legislative and enforcement authority. Instead, a new cast of actors steps onto the global stage – non-state entities that demand recognition and representation. The very fabric of sovereignty, woven with the threads of exclusive state control, becomes intertwined with the aspirations and influence of these non-state actors.

This emergence of transnational regulatory regimes marks a transformative inflection point, underscoring a fundamental reorientation in the governance landscape. The exclusive dominion of states as legislators and enforcers is challenged by these non-state actors' collaborative endeavors. As specialized regimes delve into issues ranging from climate change and human rights to trade and finance, the traditional contours of sovereign autonomy undergo a profound evolution.

Yet, this evolution raises many questions that resonate at the core of global governance. Does the ascent of non-state regulatory bodies herald a paradigmatic shift – a departure from the time-honored traditions of sovereign constitutional autonomy? Could this proliferation spell the eventual marginalization of the state as the primary locus of authority? The allure of a globally interconnected world, where transnational issues transcend national borders, casts a shadow over the primacy of the traditional sovereign state.

In this unfolding narrative, sovereignty confronts a crossroads where tradition intersects with innovation, and the age-old precepts of statehood converge with the imperatives of a borderless reality. The proliferation of specialized regimes serves as a testament to the malleability of sovereignty in the face of an interconnected world. The threads of the traditional tapestry unravel not in disarray but in a new pattern that acknowledges the role of non-state actors, embraces collaborative governance, and envisions a future where sovereignty and global interdependence coexist in a harmonious symphony of progress.

Globalization's Imprint: Redefining Sovereignty

The intensification of human interactions propelled by globalization's inexorable tide presents an inescapable reality – a subtle yet profound redefinition of sovereignty. The consensus is undeniable: the eroding effect of global forces on the sanctity of national borders is an irreversible facet of our time. The once-unassailable bastion of state sovereignty must recalibrate its coordinates in response to the emergent global dynamics.

As the transnational realm expands, as non-state actors reshape the landscape of international law, and as specialized regulatory regimes encroach upon domestic policy arenas, the very essence of sovereignty is subject to metamorphosis. While the sanctity of sovereign states remains, its contours have become malleable, adapting to the challenges of a borderless world. The future is rife with possibilities – a recalibration of power dynamics, a reimagining of governance structures, and redefining the fundamental relationships underpinning our global tapestry.

In this era of interconnectedness, the shifting dynamics of sovereignty serve as a clarion call for introspection and adaptation. The traditional dichotomy between national autonomy and international cooperation is no longer a stark binary; it has evolved into a spectrum of collaborative possibilities. As we navigate this landscape, we are presented with an opportunity to transcend traditional paradigms and embrace the fluidity of sovereignty.

The globalized world beckons nations and non-state actors to forge innovative partnerships, shape responsible transnational frameworks, and collectively address the pressing challenges that traverse national borders. The emergence of a redefined sovereignty invites a nuanced exploration – a journey that traverses the intricate interplay between self-rule and shared responsibility, autonomy, and interdependence. This is the landscape where the evolution of sovereignty finds its canvas, offering a rich tapestry upon which the collective destinies of nations, actors, and humanity are interwoven.

BALANCING SOVEREIGNTY WITH THE NECESSITY OF INTERNATIONAL COOPERATION

In global affairs, sovereignty emerges as a twin beacon – a steadfast guardian of national identity and a linchpin of the worldwide tapestry. However, the world stage now unfolds against unprecedented interconnectivity and shared trials, heralding the clarion call for international cooperation. This call paints a canvas where sovereignty and collaboration perform an intricate dance, striking a harmonious chord between self-rule and global camaraderie.

Imagine the dance floor – a global stage where nations whirl and twirl, each performing a unique dance of sovereignty. In this era, marked by intertwined destinies and shared challenges, international cooperation steps to the center, inviting sovereignty to join in a symphony of global unity. The rhythm of equilibrium is where sovereignty waltzes alongside collaboration, recognizing that the greater good often beckons nations to dance together.

The Imperative of International Cooperation

While sovereignty is a cornerstone of statehood, the rising crescendo of challenges that gracefully sweep national boundaries calls for a harmonious shift. In the grand orchestration of global affairs, a harmonious melody emerges that resonates with the profound interconnectivity of our shared destiny. The world's stage is adorned with challenges as grand as climate change, haunting as pandemics, discordant as terrorism, and as intricate as economic interdependence. These symphonic challenges transcend the confines of solitary nations, harmonizing their notes into a unified anthem of humanity's interlinked fate.

In this melodic tapestry, the chorus of international cooperation becomes an essential refrain. The realization dawns that the well-being of each nation is harmoniously woven into the well-being of all, like notes coalescing to form a symphony. The essence of sovereignty encounters a harmonious duet with collaborative endeavors, for it is only through harmonizing nations' efforts that the symphony of collective prosperity can truly be orchestrated. The confines of sovereignty find their limits when confronted by the grand crescendo of crises that elude unilateral resolutions.

The symphony of international cooperation is not just a mere partnership but an acknowledgment of our shared resonance in the grand opera of existence. It is an ode to the interconnectedness that binds nations, cultures, and lives, harmonizing their destinies into a melodic unity. As the symphony unfolds, the world witnesses the harmony that arises when nations lend their unique timbres to the collective orchestration, crafting a harmonious resonance that reverberates through the corridors of history. In this symphony of shared destiny, the imperative of international cooperation rings true – a timeless melody that sings the song of a united world striving for harmony amid the discordant challenges of our age.

Sovereignty and International Law

The interaction between sovereignty and international law unveils a nuanced equilibrium where states negotiate the complex terrain of self-governance and global collaboration. Picture this as a delicate tightrope walk, where each step signifies a nation's sovereign identity and commitment to a harmonious global order. This intricate interplay reflects the essence of international relations, a continuous quest for equilibrium between a nation's autonomous expression and its role within a broader international context.

Like skillful navigators, sovereign states chart their course through a series of agreements and treaties intertwined with the framework of international norms. These legal agreements serve as interconnected nodes, aligning to address challenges that transcend borders. Similar to a puzzle coming together, these treaties unite states, forming a network of cooperation that extends beyond national boundaries.

The elegance of this interplay lies in its equilibrium – a delicate blend between asserting a nation's independence and recognizing the value of collaborative governance. Within this intricate tapestry, states uphold their distinct characteristics while acknowledging the significance of relinquishing certain aspects of sovereignty for collective welfare. Much like a complex jigsaw puzzle, where each piece contributes to the final picture, sovereign states contribute to the collaborative mosaic of global governance.

A significant component of this dynamic is the International Criminal Court, an institution dedicated to upholding justice on an international scale. This court transcends geographical confines, acting as a beacon of impartiality in addressing cases of genocide and war crimes. Its presence illustrates the interaction of international law beyond the boundaries of individual sovereignty, underlining the notion that justice transcends territorial limitations.

Like a delicate dance, the interplay between sovereignty and international law builds to a thought-provoking climax, resonating across the global stage. It showcases the adeptness of sovereign states in balancing their autonomy with their role in a shared world. As this intricate interaction unfolds, it reveals a compelling narrative of collaboration, mutual comprehension, and the aspiration for a global framework that respects state sovereignty and global challenges' interconnected nature.

Transnational Issues (Catalysts for Cooperation)

Transnational issues, those intricate challenges that traverse borders, act as potent catalysts illuminating the inherent fragility of traditional sovereignty in a world tightly interlinked by intricate networks. These challenges, ranging from the ominous shadow of environmental degradation to the subtle yet pervasive specter of cyber threats, serve as a stark reminder that the boundaries of nation-states often blur in the face of interconnected crises.

Among these challenges, the Paris Agreement on climate change emerges as a striking exemplar of cooperative efforts that extend beyond borders. As nations converge to combat the looming specter of a global climate crisis, their collaboration underscores the inextricable interconnectedness of our shared fate. In this intricate web of cooperation, the importance of shared responsibility takes center stage, weaving together the interests and concerns of diverse nations into a unified tapestry of action.

This paradigm shift highlights the imperativeness of collective action, emphasizing that the challenges that cross borders demand responses that transcend them. In this context, sovereignty remains a guiding principle of self-governance, yet its manifestation shifts. It becomes an instrument wielded in harmony with global endeavors, a tool nations leverage to address pressing concerns collaboratively.

These instances showcase the metamorphosis of sovereignty from a solitary fortress into a vessel of collaboration, navigating the tumultuous waters of interconnected challenges. It demonstrates that while the concept of sovereignty endures, its application evolves to suit the demands of a world inextricably linked by shared vulnerabilities. As nations unite to tackle transnational issues, they create a symphony of cooperation, with sovereignty providing the melody that resonates through the intricate chords of global collaboration.

The Role of International Organizations

Intergovernmental organizations (IGOs) and international nongovernmental organizations (INGOs) emerge as crucial intermediaries, skillfully navigating the delicate balance between sovereignty and the imperative of cooperation. Think of them as diplomats on the global stage, adeptly bridging the gap between a nation's autonomous pursuits and the collective harmony sought through collaborative efforts.

The United Nations is a prime example, offering a forum where nations congregate, engage in dialogue, and forge collective pathways. It serves as a grand arena for negotiation, where the symphony of diverse voices harmonizes to address multifaceted global challenges. Here, sovereignty takes on a new role – not merely as an isolated entity but as a part of a larger ensemble, with each note contributing to the resonating chorus of international cooperation.

The World Health Organization (WHO) embodies this delicate balance, intricately weaving the threads of sovereignty and collaboration in global health. When health crises emerge, transcending national boundaries, the WHO orchestrates a response that embraces the collective might of nations. This harmonious collaboration underscores that while nations retain their sovereignty, they can harmonize their efforts despite shared threats, creating a cadence of unified action.

In this orchestration, IGOs and INGOs become conductors, guiding the symphony of diplomacy, dialogue, and joint initiatives. They recognize that while sovereignty remains an intrinsic aspect of statehood, it can harmonize with the collective aspirations of humanity. These organizations play a pivotal role in crafting a symphony where the resonance of individual sovereignty complements the harmonious chords of global cooperation, ultimately creating a composition that strives for a harmonious and interconnected world.

Economic Interdependence

Economic interdependence stands as a pragmatic balancing act, where the threads of globalization intricately weave the destinies of nations together, reshaping the traditional notions of complete sovereignty in economic realms. This transformation is akin to a tapestry interwoven with threads of trade agreements, regional economic blocs, and the intricate workings of multinational corporations that seamlessly traverse national boundaries. In this evolving narrative, pursuing economic prosperity requires nations to navigate the delicate tension between asserting sovereign autonomy and embracing the reality of shared benefits.

The rise of economic globalization has imbued the world with a sense of interconnectedness that challenges the idea of economic sovereignty in isolation. Trade agreements become more than just commercial contracts; they represent bridges between nations, fostering collaboration and exchange. Regional economic blocs, exemplified by initiatives such as the European Union, demonstrate a harmonious interplay where economic cooperation coexists with preserving national identities. In this harmonious orchestration, sovereign states elegantly move in sync with the melody of mutual growth, acknowledging that while they uphold their distinct tunes, the unified harmony produces enhanced prosperity.

The European Union's economic integration serves as a vivid illustration of this harmonization. While retaining their sovereign identities, member states collaborate closely to streamline trade, currency, and policies. This collaborative venture showcases the synergy of sovereignty and cooperation, proving that economic interdependence is not a threat to state identity but a pathway to shared growth.

In this symphony of economic interdependence, nations are akin to musicians playing distinct instruments within an orchestra. Each contributes its unique timbre, creating a harmonious composition that resonates globally. While still present, economic sovereignty adapts to the evolving landscape, embracing the reality that collaboration often yields more robust and sustainable outcomes than isolation. As the world marches forward, the pragmatic balancing act of economic interdependence redefines sovereignty's contours, spotlighting the potential for collaborative endeavors to yield symphonies of shared economic benefits.

Security and Defense

The realm of security and defense unveils a complex tapestry that interlaces sovereignty with the necessity of cooperation, illuminating the intricate balance required in a globalized context. It's a tableau where the threads of sovereign autonomy merge with the fabric of collaborative security arrangements, symbolized by military alliances such as NATO. This dynamic underscores that while complete sovereignty remains essential, the realities of shared security imperatives compel nations to navigate a nuanced dance between autonomy and cooperation.

Military alliances stand as vivid exemplars of this equilibrium. These alliances form a symphony of collective defense, wherein nations pool their resources and strengths to safeguard their shared security interests. This symphonic collaboration is not an erosion of sovereignty but a harmonization, recognizing that security threats transcend borders and necessitate united action. The North Atlantic Treaty, which obliges member states to come to each other's aid in times of need, embodies this synergy, signifying that in defense matters, the traditional boundaries of sovereignty are intertwined with the collective safety net of cooperation.

In this narrative, sovereignty is not discarded but redefined – it becomes a conscious choice to uphold national identity while recognizing that security concerns often surpass territorial confines. Nations, akin to musicians in an orchestra, each contribute their distinct notes to create a powerful composition that resonates with shared protection. This harmonious convergence showcases the adaptability of sovereignty in a globalized world, where defense collaboration enhances security without negating autonomy.

As security and defense forge a symphony of sovereignty and cooperation, it paints a vibrant canvas where nations acknowledge the complexities of an interconnected world. In this composition, sovereign autonomy harmonizes with collective action, composing a melody that resonates with the imperative of safeguarding shared security interests in an era where global challenges are increasingly intricate and interwoven.

Cultural Diplomacy

Cultural diplomacy is a profound testament to the fact that sovereignty exists not in isolation but alongside the rich tapestry of cultural diversity. Imagine this as a bridge that spans across nations, connecting the realms of identity and understanding. In a world marked by its kaleidoscope of cultures, sovereignty is interwoven with the vital pursuit of nurturing intercultural comprehension.

Like an exchange of musical notes, international cultural exchanges orchestrate a harmonious dialogue that transcends national borders.

Educational collaborations are classrooms without walls, where knowledge flows freely and enriches the collective understanding of the world's diverse narratives. People-to-people connections, akin to a dance of conversations, enable individuals to engage directly and dispel stereotypes, promoting harmony beyond geographical divides.

Preserving world heritage sites, championed by organizations like UNESCO, is a vivid embodiment of cultural diplomacy's resonance. Here, sovereignty collaborates with the collective aspiration to safeguard humanity's shared history. These sites, bearing the imprints of civilizations' past, become reminders that cultures, like notes in a melody, harmonize to create a symphony that echoes across time and space.

In this symphony of cultural diplomacy, sovereignty becomes a participant that contributes its unique motif while harmonizing with the overarching goal of fostering understanding. Diplomacy evolves from state-to-state negotiations to a symposium of cultures, where each participant contributes to a harmonious discourse that transcends political confines.

Cultural diplomacy bridges the gap between sovereignty and the interconnected world, illustrating that a nation's autonomy can coexist harmoniously with the celebration of diversity. It is a reminder that the grand tapestry of humanity's myriad cultures enriches the world, creating a mosaic where sovereignty's chords blend seamlessly with the collective melody of shared human experience.

Human Rights and Humanitarian Interventions

The intersection of human rights and humanitarian interventions unfurls a complex ethical tapestry, where the principle of sovereignty grapples with the imperative of preventing gross human rights violations. It's a scenario akin to a moral tightrope, where a nation's autonomy threads are interwoven with the universal call for protecting human dignity.

When human rights violations cast their shadow within a nation's borders, the sanctity of sovereignty faces a formidable ethical challenge. Here, the notion of sovereignty encounters a fork in the road, where the path of non-interference confronts the moral obligation to prevent atrocities. This tension between autonomy and responsibility is where the concept of humanitarian interventions takes center stage.

Humanitarian operations show a strong commitment to maintaining human lives and align with the tenets of the Responsibility to Protect (R2P) doctrine.

This principle emphasizes that sovereignty entails an intrinsic responsibility to ensure the rights and welfare of a country's inhabitants. This duty transcends borders, as the international community recognizes that the shared commitment to human dignity supersedes territorial boundaries.

The intricate balance lies in navigating this moral dichotomy. The challenge is to uphold a sovereign state's integrity while fulfilling the international community's commitment to preventing egregious human rights violations. The art of this balance is akin to a delicate dance, where the steps reflect the delicate equilibrium between respecting a nation's autonomy and preserving the sanctity of human lives.

In this dynamic, sovereignty transforms from an insular concept to a guardian of human rights. It becomes an instrument nations wield to uphold their citizens' well-being while participating in a global endeavor to prevent atrocities. While treading on sensitive ground, humanitarian interventions represent a harmonization of these objectives. In this harmonious interplay, the chords of sovereignty resonate with the universal call for safeguarding the inherent dignity of every individual, regardless of borders.

Emerging Challenges

The dawn of the digital age introduces a new dimension to sovereignty, where emerging challenges in cyberspace and outer space push the boundaries of traditional state autonomy. This evolution can be likened to a voyage into uncharted territory, where virtual and cosmic frontiers bring forth intricate questions that challenge established norms.

In cyberspace, the intangible nature of cyberattacks transcends geographical confines, rendering conventional sovereignty frameworks inadequate. The interconnectedness of our digital world necessitates a global collaboration to safeguard digital infrastructures. This endeavor mirrors a symphony of nations, harmonizing their efforts to shield against threats that can originate from anywhere, blurring the lines between national borders and demanding a collective response.

Similarly, exploring outer space propels the concept of sovereignty beyond Earth's atmosphere, prompting the emergence of cosmic diplomacy. As humanity's reach extends to the cosmos, new questions arise about property rights, resource extraction, and peaceful exploration. The Outer Space Treaty emerges as a beacon in this pursuit, emphasizing the interplay between state sovereignty and the aspiration for a peaceful and shared cosmic realm.

The evolving narrative of sovereignty in these domains speaks to the interconnected nature of our world. It underscores the imperative of collaborative engagement, where nations navigate the complexities of emerging challenges through a symphony of cooperation. Just as the orchestra harmonizes diverse instruments to create a unified melody, sovereignty in the digital and cosmic spheres harmonizes individual state interests with the collective goal of securing cyberspace and preserving the pristine expanse of outer space for the benefit of all humanity.

The art of balancing sovereignty with the necessity of international cooperation requires deft navigation. Sovereignty remains the bedrock of state identity, but the imperatives of a shared world beckon nations to collaborate. The delicate equilibrium entails recognizing that sovereignty is not a static fortress but a dynamic force harmonizing with global interdependence. As the world grapples with challenges that transcend borders, the fusion of sovereignty and cooperation creates a symphony that celebrates diversity, seeks common ground, and envisions a future where nations stand united to forge a path toward a better world.

THE IMPACTS OF EXTERNAL INFLUENCES ON NATIONAL SOVEREIGNTY

National sovereignty has stood as a fundamental pillar of international relations, representing a nation's self-governing authority over its internal and external affairs. However, the landscape in which this concept operates has evolved dramatically in our modern era of unprecedented global connectivity and interdependence. Many external influences now confront the notion of national sovereignty, each exerting a distinct impact on a nation's autonomy, decision-making processes, and overall governance.

One of the most prominent external influences reshaping national sovereignty is the phenomenon of economic globalization. Characterized by the seamless movement of goods, services, capital, and information across international borders, economic globalization has unleashed transformative effects on the global economy. Its positive facets are evident in the remarkable economic growth and enhanced living standards experienced by numerous nations. Yet, intertwined with these benefits are intricate challenges that test the boundaries of national sovereignty.

Global supply chains and financial networks have woven an intricate web that connects nations inextricably to one another. This interdependence leaves countries vulnerable to economic shocks originating far beyond their borders. The aftermath of the 2008 financial crisis vividly illustrates how external economic forces can disrupt a nation's economic stability, compelling governments to relinquish control over fiscal policies to international financial institutions such as the IMF.

In tandem with this, the ascent of multinational corporations, driven by profit incentives, represents another facet of the complex interplay between globalization and national sovereignty. These corporations hold substantial sway over domestic policies and regulations, often leveraging their clout to demand concessions or exemptions from governments. This dynamic not only exemplifies the influence of external entities on a nation's sovereignty but also poses a potential threat to its capacity to enact laws aligned with its distinct socio-economic priorities. Consequently, to varying degrees, economic globalization has chipped away at the exclusive economic decision-making authority conventionally associated with national sovereignty.

A crucial illustration of the changing nature of national sovereignty is evident in international organizations. Entities like the United Nations, World Trade Organization, and World Health Organization have fostered global collaboration spanning various spheres. By providing platforms for dialogue, negotiation, and consensus-building among member states, these organizations endeavor to tackle shared challenges, including climate change, public health crises, and human rights violations. However, the cooperative nature of these endeavors introduces a distinct dimension to the sovereignty discourse.

Member states often choose to pool their sovereignty in engaging with international agreements, treaties, and conventions. While this enhances a nation's participation on the global stage, it simultaneously constrains its independent decision-making capacity. Such commitments compel adherence to rules and norms established by these organizations, as exemplified by environmental accords like the Paris Agreement. Although designed to address global concerns, these agreements can constrict a nation's autonomy by mandating the adoption of measures that may affect its domestic policies.

The proliferation of transnational threats has further blurred the lines of national sovereignty. Terrorism, cyberattacks, and organized crime transcend national borders, necessitating collaborative responses for effective mitigation. International alliances, such as NATO, allow nations to pool resources and intelligence, thereby bolstering collective security. However, this cooperation inevitably entails shared decision-making, potentially compromising a nation's absolute autonomy in responding to imminent threats.

In the cultural sphere, the effects of globalization manifest in the diffusion of ideas, values, and lifestyles facilitated by technology and media. While cultural exchange fosters intercultural understanding and dialogue, it simultaneously challenges traditional cultural identities and practices. As nations absorb foreign cultural influences, they may be compelled to conform to global norms, potentially compromising their unique identities and sovereignty.

Language, art, and traditions, which form the bedrock of national identities, are not immune to this influence. The influx of foreign media content challenges the importance of local cultural expressions, eroding a nation's ability to shape and control its cultural narrative. Moreover, the propagation of global consumerism can homogenize consumer preferences, posing a potential threat to indigenous industries and local markets.

The digital age has revolutionized communication and connectivity, ushering in unprecedented access to information and influencing public opinion. Social media platforms, for instance, empower individuals to share ideas and mobilize across borders, posing a direct challenge to governments' control over information dissemination. This has prompted some nations to resort to censorship and internet controls to maintain their narrative and suppress dissent, highlighting the intricate interplay between technological advancement and the preservation of national sovereignty.

Against these multifaceted influences, a comprehensive exploration of the impact of external forces on national sovereignty underscores a delicate equilibrium between autonomy and interconnectedness. While economic globalization and international organizations provide avenues for cooperation and collective problem-solving, they also have the potential to curtail individual decision-making authority. Transnational threats necessitate collaborative security efforts that may challenge the notion of complete control. Simultaneously, cultural diffusion and technological progress, while fostering connectivity, can also serve as catalysts for cultural transformation and information dissemination that challenges traditional sovereignty paradigms.

In this dynamic landscape, nations are tasked with balancing embracing global interconnectedness and safeguarding their unique identities and interests. The challenges posed by external influences necessitate innovative governance structures that enable nations to participate actively in the global community while preserving their core values and sovereignty. As the world evolves, the intricate relationship between external influences and national sovereignty will remain a central and ever-evolving facet of international relations.

THE COMPLEX LANDSCAPE OF INTERDEPENDENCE

In our modern era, the rising tide of interconnectedness and interdependence has given us a profound challenge - skillfully maneuvering through the intricate mesh of relationships, systems, and interactions. The notion of interdependence extends beyond the confines of geography, cultural distinctions, and economic terrains, permeating every dimension of our existence. This phenomenon resonates across diverse realms, ranging from the vast realms of global economics and intricate webs of political dynamics to the intimate domains of personal connections and the imperative of environmental sustainability. The intricate interplay of these multifaceted elements necessitates a comprehensive comprehension and a strategic, discerning approach.

Unveiling the Tapestry of Interconnectedness

Interdependence, at its core, signifies the mutual reliance and influence between individuals, groups, nations, and systems. It underscores the undeniable truth that actions in one corner of the world can trigger ripple effects that span continents. Our modern era, characterized by rapid technological advancements and communication breakthroughs, has unprecedentedly accelerated this interconnectedness. What happens in a remote village can impact the stock markets of global financial hubs, just as international trade decisions can reverberate through local communities.

The complex network of interdependence is woven from threads of various dimensions:

1. Economic Interdependence

   The global economy is a prime example of intricate interdependence. Supply chains stretch across borders, with components of products often manufactured in different countries before final assembly. A disruption in one region can lead to cascading effects that impact businesses and consumers worldwide. The 2008 financial crisis showcased how interlinked financial systems can trigger a chain reaction resulting in a widespread economic downturn.

2. Environmental Interdependence
   The health of our planet hinges on a delicate balance of ecosystems and climate patterns. The concept of interdependence is apparent in phenomena such as climate change, wherein emissions from a single nation can play a role in causing increased sea levels and severe weather occurrences on the opposite side of the world. Collaborative efforts are essential to address environmental challenges, emphasizing the need for intergovernmental agreements and grassroots initiatives.

3. Political and Social Interdependence
   Geopolitical decisions and social movements resonate across boundaries. The Arab Spring, for instance, highlighted the power of social media in facilitating cross-border influence and inspiring similar movements globally. International diplomacy and cooperation are vital to tackling terrorism, pandemics, and human rights abuses that transcend national borders.

4. Technological Interdependence
   The digital era has introduced an unparalleled level of technological interdependence. The internet links individuals across continents, facilitating immediate communication and information sharing. The advent of artificial intelligence and automation further amplifies interdependence, as breakthroughs in one part of the world can reshape industries and labor markets worldwide.

The Ripple Effect: Interdependence in Action

Interdependence manifests in myriad ways, often with far-reaching consequences beyond initial actions. Let's explore some examples that illustrate the ripple effect of interconnectedness:

- Global Supply Chains and the Butterfly Effect
  The COVID-19 pandemic underscored the vulnerability of global supply chains. Factory shutdowns in one country disrupted the production of goods worldwide, leading to shortages of essential items. The interconnected nature of supply chains demonstrates how localized disruptions can trigger a domino effect, affecting industries and economies globally.

- Climate Migration and Resource Scarcity
  Environmental changes, exacerbated by human activity, can trigger global migration patterns. The escalation of sea levels and occurrences of severe weather can result in the displacement of communities, giving rise to social and political complications in both the places of origin and the receiving nations. This underscores the intricate interaction among environmental, social, and political elements.

- Financial Contagion and Market Dynamics
  The vulnerability of interlinked financial systems was laid bare by the 1997 Asian financial crisis and the 2008 global financial crisis. A crisis originating in one nation has the potential to trigger contagion, wherein investor anxiety transcends borders, impacting economies and markets well beyond the initial point of impact. This underscores the need for international cooperation in financial regulation and crisis management.

Navigating the Interdependent Terrain

As we navigate through the intricate terrain of interdependence, a multitude of strategies and approaches arise to guide us through the challenges it presents and to seize the opportunities it offers:

1. Collaborative Diplomacy
   Effective diplomacy is essential in a world where decisions made by one nation can have widespread ramifications. International

treaties, agreements, and forums provide platforms for nations to collaborate on issues such as disarmament, climate change, and trade. Diplomatic efforts promote understanding, mitigate conflicts, and pave the way for coordinated action.

2. Multilateral Institutions
   Organizations like the United Nations, World Trade Organization, and International Monetary Fund play crucial roles in fostering cooperation and managing interdependence. These institutions provide frameworks for dialogue, negotiation, and conflict resolution, helping to prevent global issues from escalating into crises.

3. Sustainable Development Goal
   The UN's Sustainable Development Goals (SDGs) recognize the interconnected nature of the world's concerns.

   By tackling concerns like poverty, inequality, and environmental degradation, the SDGs aspire to establish a more balanced and sustainable world. Achieving these goals requires collaboration across borders and sectors.

4. Resilient Systems and Redundancy
   Building resilience into interconnected systems is essential to mitigate the impact of disruptions. Diversifying supply chains, investing in local industries, and creating redundancy in critical infrastructure can enhance a society's ability to withstand shocks and maintain stability.

5. Digital Literacy and Ethical Tech Development
   In the era of technological interdependence, fostering digital literacy and responsible tech development is paramount. Education and awareness campaigns can empower individuals to navigate the

digital landscape safely and ethically, while international agreements can establish data privacy and cybersecurity norms.

The Power of Individual Agency

While the complex landscape of interdependence may seem overwhelming, individual agency remains a potent force. Each person can contribute positively to the global community and shape the outcomes of interconnected systems. Here's how:

- Informed Citizenship
  Engage with current affairs and global issues to make informed decisions as a citizen. Stay abreast of developments, seek diverse perspectives, and participate in civic activities that promote positive change.

- Cultural Intelligence
  Develop an understanding of different cultures, beliefs, and values. Embrace diversity and practice empathy to foster mutual respect and cooperation in an interconnected world.

- Sustainable Practices
  Adopt sustainable habits in daily life to reduce environmental impact. Conserving resources, minimizing waste, and supporting eco-friendly initiatives contribute to a healthier planet.

- Digital Responsibility
  Practice ethical behavior in the digital realm. Respect online privacy, engage in civil discourse, and leverage technology for constructive purposes.

- Social Entrepreneurship
  Channel entrepreneurial spirit towards addressing societal challenges. Through the development of inventive solutions, social

entrepreneurs can enact beneficial transformations and serve as sources of inspiration for others to emulate.

Navigating the complex landscape of interdependence is a journey of understanding, adaptation, and collaboration. Recognizing the intricate web of relationships and systems is essential for informed decision-making and meaningful progress as our world becomes increasingly interconnected. We can collectively steer the course toward a more harmonious and resilient global community by embracing collaborative diplomacy principles, harnessing multilateral institutions' power, and fostering individual agency. Interdependence, with its challenges and opportunities, invites us to rise above borders and boundaries, uniting in pursuit of a shared future.

CHAPTER TWO

THE NEED FOR BETTER ECONOMIC GLOBAL ARCHITECTURE

Economic global architecture, a term often used interchangeably with the global economic order, refers to the intricate framework that governs the complex interactions, relationships, and systems within the global economy. This comprehensive structure encompasses many components, including international trade agreements, financial institutions, regulatory frameworks, multinational corporations, and currency exchange mechanisms. Together, these elements define the rules, norms, and mechanisms that shape the behavior of nations, businesses, and individuals engaged in cross-border economic activities.

A level of interdependence and interconnectedness unparalleled in human history characterizes the modern world. The global economy has transformed into a tightly woven tapestry of interactions as goods, services, information, and capital flow seamlessly across borders. At the heart of this intricate web lies the concept of economic global architecture—an intricate framework that dictates the rules of engagement, the flow of resources, and the dynamics of economic relationships on a global scale.

This architecture is the foundational structure upon which the complex edifice of international trade, finance, and economic cooperation is built. It establishes the parameters for how nations interact economically, influencing everything from trade agreements and investment policies to financial regulations and exchange rate mechanisms. As a result, the economic global architecture plays a pivotal role in shaping the economic fortunes of nations, determining the winners and losers in the global marketplace.

However, as the world continues to evolve, the existing economic global architecture finds itself at a crossroads. The challenges and opportunities presented by technological advancements, shifting geopolitical landscapes, and pressing environmental concerns underscore the need for a more adaptive, inclusive, and equitable framework. The imperative for improvement has become evident, as the current architecture must accommodate these changes and harness their potential for the betterment of all.

This chapter delves into the intricate nuances of global economic architecture. We explore its various components and mechanisms, dissect its challenges in the modern era, and examine the compelling reasons for its transformation. We aim to illuminate the path toward a more resilient, sustainable, and prosperous global economic order through a comprehensive analysis of the forces at play. As we navigate the uncharted waters of an increasingly interdependent world, the call for a revamped economic global architecture becomes not just a necessity but a beacon guiding us toward a future of shared prosperity and collective progress.

CURRENT FLAWS IN THE GLOBAL ECONOMIC SYSTEM

Amidst the intricate weave of human history, the global economic system emerges as an influential cornerstone, molding the trajectories of both nations and individuals. Interwoven within this intricate fabric are the strands of trade, finance, and interconnections, intricately stitching visions of prosperity and advancement across geographical boundaries. Yet, hidden within these intricacies are flaws that cast a shadow over its aspiration for fair prosperity and collective welfare. As we embark on a journey to expose these imperfections, a realm emerges where equality among nations wavers, compelling nations to grapple with the weight of discrepancies resonating across their economies and societies.

The Mirage of Equality

Deep within the intricate framework of the global economic system, an illusory mirage of equality captures the imagination – a captivating vision of harmonious growth and collective rewards. This shimmering promise, akin to an oasis on the horizon, allures an equitable world order where every nation has an equal opportunity to thrive. However, as one ventures further into this intricate tapestry, the veil of illusion gradually lifts, revealing a landscape that starkly contrasts with the illusion.

The initial allure of this mirage fades as one confronts the reality of a world characterized by profound inequities. The fervent hope for a level playing field where nations, irrespective of their status, can ascend the ladder of prosperity stands in stark contrast to the prevailing truth. Far from fostering a fair terrain, the global economic system often perpetuates and even exacerbates existing disparities. Instead of functioning as an equalizer, it sometimes becomes a magnifier, amplifying some advantages while relegating others to the periphery.

In this landscape of economic intricacies, the promise of shared benefits remains elusive for many. Rather than acting as a catalyst for universal growth, the current system inadvertently sustains the asymmetry of opportunities. Nations with historical advantages are often better positioned to harness the benefits of global trade and investment, allowing them to soar to greater heights. Meanwhile, those that have been historically marginalized find themselves trapped in the shadows, struggling to secure a foothold on the ladder of progress.

The mirage of equality in the global economic system is a stark reminder of the complexity underpinning our interconnected world. It challenges us to delve beyond surface appearances and acknowledge the underlying disparities that shape the destinies of nations. Recognizing the imperfections of this mirage, we are compelled to explore avenues that lead to genuine inclusivity and equitable growth. We can only aspire to transform this mirage into a tangible reality of shared prosperity for all nations through a concerted effort to address these inherent flaws.

Flawed Trade Dynamics

Trade, the pulsating lifeblood of the global economy, possesses a dual nature, harboring the potential for both expansion and inequality. The intricate mechanisms governing trade dynamics, conceived to facilitate the seamless flow of commodities and services, can unwittingly tip the scales in favor of those already endowed. Dominant economies wield their influence adeptly, negotiating terms that favor their interests, thus leaving smaller nations grappling with the daunting task of competing on an unbalanced battleground.

Amidst this backdrop, the ominous trio of tariffs, subsidies, and non-tariff barriers emerges as formidable gatekeepers. These barriers, ostensibly erected to regulate trade, can inadvertently become tools of exclusion, relegating developing countries to the sidelines of profitable markets. The consequence impedes their economic growth, trapping them in a cycle of reliance on more advantaged nations. The inherent flaw in these trade dynamics perpetuates a system where opportunities are skewed, and aspirations are stifled. It is imperative to recalibrate the balance for a more equitable global trade landscape.

The Debt Dilemma

Within the fold of the global economic system's embrace, not all nations are met with warmth; for many, it brings the burden of suffocating debt. As developing countries strive to carve their niche on the global stage, they often become entangled in a complex web of loans extended by affluent nations and international financial bodies. Initially offered to propel growth, these loans can swiftly transform into a vice-like grip, diverting essential resources away from critical social services and vital infrastructure endeavors.

This web of indebtedness casts a shadow on a nation's potential, ensnaring it in a cycle that perpetuates economic inertia. The ceaseless cycle of repaying debt stifles the room for maneuverability, hindering the capacity to invest in areas that drive genuine progress. The debt dilemma not only undermines a country's prospects for self-reliance but also threatens its ability to ascend beyond the confines of its circumstances. Addressing this dilemma is imperative to unshackling nations from the clutches of debt and unlocking their potential for sustained and inclusive development.

Financial Volatility and Fragility

Amidst the towering edifices of global financial hubs, a tempest of volatility frequently simmers, its reverberations extend well past national boundaries. The intricate interlinkages between financial markets, despite enabling swift streams of capital, concurrently lay bare nations to the perilous specter of contagion. A crisis brewing in a distant corner of the globe holds the potential to cascade like a chain reaction, casting economies into tumult across continents. This tumultuous instability poses the greatest threat to developing nations, as their constrained resources and fragile financial frameworks render them defenseless against external shocks.

In this intricate dance of global finance, even minor ripples can evolve into surging waves of disruption. The phenomenon underscores the imperative of building resilience within financial systems, ensuring that even the most vulnerable nations possess the mechanisms to weather the storm. As the world becomes increasingly interconnected, addressing the intricacies of financial volatility becomes an integral facet of nurturing equitable global prosperity.

Technological Disruption and Inequality

The digital age, with its promises of innovation and progress, also casts a shadow of inequality. Technological advancements, while transforming industries and economies, can exacerbate existing disparities. The digital divide, characterized by unequal access to technology and information, creates a chasm between nations that can harness the benefits of the digital revolution and those left on the fringes. Automation threatens jobs in developing economies, further deepening inequalities and posing challenges to sustainable development.

Environmental Exploitation and Disparities

As the global economic system powers forward, it often does so at the expense of the environment, perpetuating a cycle of ecological degradation that disproportionately impacts vulnerable nations. Extractive industries, unchecked pollution, and resource depletion can devastate ecosystems and communities, hitting developing countries the hardest. These nations bear the brunt of environmental crises, which can lead to displacement, loss of livelihoods, and social unrest, further entrenching inequalities.

A Call for Equitable Change

A rallying cry for change resonates amid the flaws that mar the current global economic system. The imperative for equitable global prosperity has never been stronger. Recognizing the interconnectedness of nations and humanity's shared destiny, there is a growing momentum to address these flaws and forge a path toward a more just and inclusive economic order.

Balancing Trade and Development

A cornerstone of equitable change lies in reimagining trade dynamics. A recalibration of trade agreements to prioritize sustainable development and the needs of developing nations is essential. The global economic system can foster a more level playing field by reducing trade barriers, addressing subsidies that distort markets, and providing technical assistance. Fair and transparent trade practices can empower nations to harness their comparative advantages and participate more meaningfully in the global economy.

Debt Relief and Sustainable Financing

Addressing the debt dilemma requires a comprehensive approach that balances financial stability with sustainable development. Initiatives for debt relief and adopting responsible lending practices offer developing nations the opportunity to allocate resources to vital sectors like education, healthcare, and infrastructure. By embracing inventive financing mechanisms like impact investing and green bonds, resources can be directed toward endeavors that foster economic growth and environmental sustainability.

Strengthening Financial Resilience

Enhancing financial stability is pivotal to mitigating the impact of financial volatility on developing nations. The global economic system can foster resilience by promoting responsible lending and borrowing practices, bolstering financial regulation, and ensuring financial institutions are accountable for their actions. Mechanisms for crisis prevention and management can provide a safety net, shielding nations from the destructive aftermath of economic shocks.

Harnessing Technology for Inclusion

When harnessed thoughtfully, technology can bridge gaps and create pathways to inclusion. Initiatives to expand digital infrastructure, improve access to education and training, and promote technological innovation in developing nations can pave the way for more equitable participation in the digital economy. Collective endeavors between developed and developing nations play a pivotal role in guaranteeing that the advantages of technology extend to even the most remote corners of the world.

Sustainable Development and Environmental Justice

A commitment to environmental sustainability is central to achieving equitable global prosperity. The global economic system can drive change by incentivizing sustainable practices, promoting clean technologies, and supporting nations in transitioning to green economies. International cooperation on environmental agreements, climate adaptation, and resource management can ensure that the burdens and benefits of environmental stewardship are shared equitably.

Empowering Local Initiatives

Ultimately, the pursuit of equitable global prosperity rests on empowering local initiatives and nurturing homegrown solutions. Grassroots efforts, community-driven development projects, and social entrepreneurship can empower individuals and communities to shape their destinies. The global economic system can be supportive by providing resources, expertise, and collaboration platforms that amplify these local endeavors' impact.

The imperfections within the present global economic system are indisputable, yet so is the capacity for transformation. The vision of a fair global prosperity edges closer to realization as nations, communities, and individuals unite to tackle these imperfections. The global economic system can evolve into a force that propels all nations towards shared well-being by recalibrating trade dynamics, fostering sustainable financing, strengthening financial resilience, harnessing technology, prioritizing environmental justice, and empowering local initiatives. The quest for equitable global prosperity is a journey fraught with challenges but also a journey that holds the promise of a brighter and more inclusive future for all.

PURSUING ECONOMIC ARCHITECTURE THAT FOSTERS EQUALITY AND INCLUSION

Imagine a world where the concept of "us" and "them" dissolves into a symphony of collaboration, where the aspirations of a small village in one corner of the globe resonate with the ambitions of a bustling metropolis in another. This vision drives the pursuit of economic architecture that fosters equality and inclusion – a vision where every nation is afforded a seat at the table of progress, regardless of its historical narrative or geographical coordinates.

At the heart of this transformation lies visionary leadership, leaders who rise above the tide of short-term gains to navigate the uncharted waters of long-term, sustainable growth. The shackles of conventional wisdom do not bind these leaders; they are the trailblazers who envision an economic landscape that thrives on the principles of fairness and shared destiny. Their decisions, guided by a moral compass, breathe life into policies that prioritize investments in education, social welfare, and infrastructure, recognizing that the dividends of such investments far outweigh the allure of fleeting gains.

Yet, the journey towards a more inclusive economic architecture requires more than just visionary leadership; it necessitates a paradigm shift in the mechanisms underpinning global trade and investment. It beckons leaders to dismantle the walls of trade barriers that have long stifled the potential of developing nations. Envision a situation where tariffs, previously used as obstacles, transform into bridges of potential, permitting the seamless exchange of goods and services across borders and unveiling fresh pathways for expansion. Such an approach doesn't just level the playing field; it transforms it into fertile ground for innovation, entrepreneurship, and shared prosperity.

In this new economic narrative, investment is not a privilege reserved for the affluent but a lifeline extended to all nations, irrespective of their economic prowess. World leaders collaborate to design investment frameworks that empower emerging economies, nurturing a diverse ecosystem of startups, businesses, and industries. This approach breathes life into regions that were once marginalized, spurring job creation, technological advancement, and a sense of ownership in the global economic tapestry.

Still, the path toward an inclusive economic architecture encounters obstacles, with financing emerging as a pivotal concern. In this context, innovation emerges as the guiding star, directing leaders toward sustainable resolutions. Picture a world where international funds, buoyed by a collective commitment, flow toward eradicating poverty, combating climate change, and advancing education. These funds stand as a testament to the shared determination of nations, evolving into tools of transformation that cultivate a fairer distribution of resources and opportunities.

Education stands as a cornerstone of empowerment, a key that unlocks the doors to economic inclusion. Leaders collaborate to establish global education initiatives that transcend geographical boundaries, bringing knowledge to every corner of the world. Imagine a scenario where digital literacy programs, vocational training, and quality education are accessible to even the most remote communities. This commitment to education doesn't just empower individuals; it catalyzes an economic renaissance, nurturing a skilled workforce that fuels innovation and drives economic growth.

But economic inclusion goes beyond education; it extends to safeguarding the vulnerable and eradicating poverty. Here, world leaders envision comprehensive social safety nets that cradle those in need, ensuring access to healthcare, basic income support, and affordable housing. In this compassionate economic order, no one is left behind; everyone is equipped with the tools to contribute meaningfully to their society and nation's progress.

However, the quest for equality and inclusion still needs a profound dedication to environmental sustainability. World leaders come together to formulate policies that interweave economic growth with conscientious resource management, adopting renewable energy, and reducing carbon emissions. This comprehensive strategy goes beyond national concerns, acknowledging that the planet's well-being is intricately entwined with the essence of global prosperity.

Technology has become an equalizer in this new economic paradigm, bridging the gaps between nations. Leaders facilitate the transfer of technology from developed to developing nations, ensuring that innovative solutions are accessible to all. Collaborative research initiatives flourish, propelling nations towards economic diversification, entrepreneurship, and a thriving digital economy. The digital divide narrows, and the promise of technology becomes a reality for even the most remote communities.

Crucially, the pursuit of economic architecture that fosters equality and inclusion hinges on the power of collective action. World leaders forge partnerships that transcend geopolitical boundaries, uniting towards a common goal. These partnerships become conduits for knowledge sharing, resource pooling, and joint problem-solving. Imagine nations collaborating to tackle challenges that transcend borders – poverty, healthcare, education, and beyond. In this united front, the seeds of equality and inclusion take root and flourish.

As this transformative journey unfolds, leaders redefine success, moving beyond the narrow confines of GDP growth. They champion alternative metrics that measure well-being, social progress, and environmental stewardship. In this new measurement of prosperity, the value of human lives and the planet's health take center stage, guiding policies prioritizing holistic development over fleeting economic gains.

Pursuing economic architecture that fosters equality and inclusion is not a mere ideal; it is a roadmap toward a world where shared prosperity is not a distant dream but a lived reality. It is a journey that requires the collective resolve of visionary leaders, innovative policies, and global collaboration. As world leaders embrace this transformative mission, they have the power to reshape the economic landscape, knitting together a tapestry of nations where equality, inclusion, and shared well-being are not just aspirations but the very essence of a brighter future for all.

ROLE OF INTERNATIONAL INSTITUTIONS IN SHAPING EQUITABLE ECONOMIC POLICIES

In today's global economy, the role of international institutions in shaping equitable economic policies has become increasingly pivotal. These establishments, spanning from the International Monetary Fund (IMF) and World Bank to regional entities such as European Union (EU) and African Union (AU), assume a critical function in advancing economic steadiness, nurturing collaboration, and guaranteeing balanced progress among nations.

The European Union has been a pioneer in promoting social cohesion through its regional policies. The EU's Structural and Investment Funds support less-developed regions financially, fostering infrastructure development, education, and job creation. The EU contributes to more equitable economic growth within the bloc by narrowing development gaps between member states.

The IMF's PRGF program also aims to assist low-income countries in designing and implementing poverty reduction strategies. The program encourages countries to prioritize pro-poor policies through financial support and policy advice, such as investing in healthcare, education, and social safety nets.

The Significance of Equitable Economic Policies

At the heart of the global economic narrative, equitable economic policies are a lighthouse guiding nations through the tumultuous waters of development. Based on the principles of equity and impartiality, these policies act as a pivotal point around which societies harmonize their ambitions for progress while upholding the necessities of communal welfare.

The significance of equitable economic policies transcends mere rhetoric; it encapsulates a profound understanding of the intricate web of interdependencies that constitute modern economies. In a world where economic inequalities can breed social unrest and hinder progress, these policies emerge as a necessary bridge between the haves and the have-nots, forging a path toward inclusive prosperity.

Imagine a society where the benefits of economic growth cascade down every rung of the social ladder, nourishing each individual's potential and kindling the flames of hope. Equitable economic policies promise to level the playing field, breaking down barriers that inhibit marginalized communities from participating in and contributing to the economic discourse. This inclusive approach does more than just lift individuals out of poverty; it cultivates a sense of ownership, fostering a collective sense of purpose and shared destiny.

These policies serve as a potent elixir for social cohesion in a world marked by the chasm between affluence and destitution. Equitable economic policies become the glue that binds communities together by ensuring that the fruits of economic progress are not confined to a privileged few but rather are distributed among diverse segments of society. They diminish the fault lines that often give rise to social strife, forging connections across different backgrounds and beliefs.

Moreover, equitable economic policies are not mere luxuries but imperatives for long-term stability and sustainable growth. As economies expand and evolve, the absence of mechanisms to ensure the equitable distribution of benefits can lead to imbalances undermining development foundations. A lopsided distribution of wealth can amplify social tensions and erode trust in institutions, casting shadows of uncertainty over the trajectory of progress.

While the vision of equitable economic policies is compelling, their realization is a complex symphony that requires meticulous orchestration. The threads of policy formulation must be woven with a keen understanding of the intricate economic dynamics at play, avoiding unintended consequences that could stifle growth or exacerbate disparities. At the national level, governments must navigate a delicate dance between stimulating economic activity and safeguarding the interests of vulnerable populations.

However, the canvas of equitable economic policies extends beyond national borders. In our interconnected world, disparities within one nation can reverberate across the global stage, affecting trade, investment, and geopolitical stability. International coordination, facilitated by institutions, becomes crucial to harmonize efforts and prevent a race to the bottom where countries vie for economic advantages at the expense of equity.

The Role of International Institutions

1. Knowledge Dissemination and Capacity Building
   International institutions act as repositories of economic knowledge and best practices. They provide valuable research, data, and policy

recommendations to member countries, enabling them to make informed decisions. The IMF, for instance, publishes the World Economic Outlook and Fiscal Monitor reports, offering insights into global economic trends and fiscal policies. These institutions empower countries to design and implement more equitable economic policies by disseminating knowledge and facilitating capacity building.

2. Policy Coordination and Harmonization
   Equitable economic policies often require coordination and harmonization among countries to prevent the "race to the bottom" phenomenon, where nations compete by adopting lax regulations or unfair tax practices. International institutions provide a platform for dialogue and cooperation, helping countries align their policies to ensure fairness and prevent negative externalities. The Organization for Economic Cooperation and Development (OECD) is crucial in establishing global benchmarks for tax transparency and anti-corruption strategies, fostering an equitable platform for businesses, and mitigating disparities stemming from disparate regulatory landscapes.

3. Financial Assistance and Technical Support
   Due to limited resources and expertise, many developing countries need help formulating and implementing equitable economic policies. International institutions offer financial and technical support to help these countries design and execute effective policies. The World Bank funds projects promoting inclusive growth, such as education and healthcare initiatives, infrastructure development, and poverty reduction programs. These institutions contribute to reducing disparities and advancing economic equity through targeted assistance.

4. Crisis Management and Stability
   During times of economic crisis, international institutions play a crucial role in stabilizing economies and preventing social upheaval.

   For instance, the IMF provides financial aid packages to nations with currency or balance of payments issues. These packages often come with conditions that require recipient countries to implement structural reforms to enhance equity, such as reducing subsidies for the affluent and redirecting resources toward social programs. By addressing economic vulnerabilities, international institutions maintain stability and promote fair economic outcomes.

Mechanisms of Influence

The influence of international institutions on shaping equitable economic policies is realized through a variety of mechanisms:

1. Conditionality
   Financial assistance provided by international institutions often comes with conditions that recipient countries must meet to access funding. These conditions may include implementing policy reforms to promote equity, such as improving social safety nets or increasing access to education and healthcare. Conditionality ensures that countries adopt measures that contribute to more equitable economic outcomes.

2. Policy Advice and Technical Expertise
   International institutions offer policy advice and technical expertise to member countries. This guidance is based on rigorous analysis and research, helping countries design policies tailored to their unique economic circumstances. By leveraging the expertise of these institutions, countries can formulate more effective strategies for reducing inequality and promoting equitable growth.

3. Monitoring and Accountability
   International institutions monitor the implementation of economic policies and assess their impact on equity and development. Regular assessments provide a basis for feedback and accountability, enabling countries to adjust their policies if necessary. For instance, the United Nations Development Programme (UNDP) publishes the Human Development Index (HDI), which ranks countries based on income, education, and life expectancy. This index holds countries accountable for their progress in achieving equitable human development.

Challenges and Criticisms

While international institutions play a vital role in shaping equitable economic policies, they are not without challenges and criticisms:

- Democratic Deficit
  Critics argue that some international institutions lack democratic legitimacy, as a small group often makes decisions of powerful countries. This can lead to policies prioritizing these countries' interests over the needs of smaller or less influential nations, potentially exacerbating inequality.

- Policy Imposition
  International institutions' imposition of policy conditions can sometimes be seen as intrusive and insensitive to local contexts. Policymakers may perceive these conditions as undermining their sovereignty and ability to tailor policies to their specific economic and social conditions.

- Inadequate Representation
  The representation of developing nations in international organizations is frequently restricted, resulting in imbalanced priorities and policies that inadequately tackle the distinctive

difficulties confronted by these countries. This lack of representation can hinder efforts to promote equitable economic policies.

In the complex landscape of global economics, international institutions play a critical role in shaping equitable economic policies. Through knowledge dissemination, policy coordination, financial assistance, and crisis management, these institutions reduce inequality and promote sustainable development. While challenges and criticisms exist, the mechanisms and examples highlighted in this exploration demonstrate the potential of international institutions to drive positive change and create a more just and equitable world economy. As countries continue to grapple with the intricacies of economic policy, the role of these institutions remains indispensable in forging a path toward shared prosperity.

CRAFTING A BLUEPRINT FOR GLOBAL ECONOMIC REFORM

The call for global economic reform resonates with urgency and purpose in a world marked by stark economic disparities. The prevailing landscape, marred by unequal distribution of wealth, resources, and opportunities, beckons for a transformative shift towards a more equitable and harmonious future.

This narrative is not of despair but hope, which envisions a metamorphosis as profound as the seasons' changing dance. The current landscape, painted with hues of discord, holds within its every brushstroke the potential for a masterpiece that celebrates human potential and endeavor. As the pendulum of time swings, it carries with it whispers of transformation—whispers that entice the collective imagination to weave a tapestry of change, vibrant and inclusive.

The urgency of this epoch is a palpable heartbeat, quickening as societies unite in the understanding that progress cannot be measured solely in monetary terms. It is an understanding that heralds a new dawn, where economic reformation becomes the compass guiding us toward a future characterized not by divisions but by bridges spanning across continents and cultures.

We stand on the precipice of possibility with a compass and a shared purpose igniting our spirits. As we step forward, let us embrace the challenge of shaping an equitable and harmonious tomorrow, where the cadence of global economic reform harmonizes with the symphony of human potential, creating a melody that resonates for generations to come.

Unveiling the Imperative for Reform

Modern global economic architecture stands at a crossroads where the chasm between affluence and deprivation looms larger than ever before. The repercussions of these disparities are far-reaching, reverberating across continents and manifesting in myriad forms – social unrest, political instability, and ecological imbalances. The imperative for global economic reform emerges as a beacon of hope, illuminating the path toward a more just, sustainable, and cohesive world.

The Complex Web of Economic Disparities

A panoramic view of the global economic panorama reveals a complex web of disparities that extend beyond mere financial inequalities. Geographical regions, socio-economic strata, and gender divisions intertwine to create a multidimensional tapestry of disadvantage. Wealth and resources, rather than equitably shared, often concentrate within a narrow subset of nations and individuals, accentuating the divide between the privileged and the marginalized.

Crafting a Blueprint for Unity

1. Redefining Growth and Success
   The cornerstone of global economic reform lies in reimagining growth and success. Moving beyond traditional measures such as

Gross Domestic Product (GDP), a reformed economic framework should encompass well-being indicators, social progress, and environmental sustainability. This shift in perspective would recalibrate the pursuit of growth towards a more holistic and inclusive understanding of prosperity.

2. Inclusive and Equitable Policies
A blueprint for unity necessitates designing and implementing inclusive and equitable policies that address the root causes of disparities. Social safety nets, quality education, accessible healthcare, and sustainable livelihoods must be prioritized to create a level playing field for all individuals, irrespective of their socio-economic background.

3. Ethical and Responsible Business Practices
The private sector wields considerable influence over global economic dynamics. As such, a reformed economic landscape demands ethical and responsible business practices prioritizing social and environmental well-being alongside financial gains. Corporate social responsibility and sustainability initiatives must be integral to this blueprint for unity.

4. Global Trade and Cooperation
Reform on a global scale requires reimagining the dynamics of trade and cooperation. Establishing fair trade practices, minimizing trade obstacles, and fostering cooperative endeavors to tackle global issues like climate change and public health emergencies ought to serve as the foundational principles of a revamped economic framework. Multilateral institutions play a crucial role in facilitating such cooperation.

5 Empowerment of Marginalized Communities
The blueprint for unity must empower marginalized communities within and between nations. Empowerment entails fostering

entrepreneurship, promoting access to credit, and creating avenues for skill development. It is paramount to elevate the voices of underrepresented groups and integrate their perspectives into economic decision-making processes.

Overcoming Challenges on the Road to Reform

The journey towards global economic reform is fraught with challenges, requiring a steadfast commitment to navigate the intricacies:

1. Political Will and Leadership
   Reform demands strong political will and visionary leadership that transcends short-term interests. Interweaving domestic and international political forces can intricately complicate the execution of transformative actions. Global leaders must rise above geopolitical rivalries and champion the cause of unity to pave the way for reform.

2. Resistance to Change
   The inertia of established economic structures and vested interests can pose significant roadblocks to reform. Powerful stakeholders may resist relinquishing their advantages, fearing potential disruptions to their status quo. Convincing these stakeholders of the long-term benefits of reform is a formidable challenge that requires persuasive advocacy and robust evidence.

3. Coordination and Implementation
   Crafting a blueprint for unity is a nuanced endeavor that necessitates harmonizing diverse policies and perspectives. Achieving consensus among nations with varying economic, cultural, and political contexts demands adept diplomacy and effective coordination. Implementing reforms consistently and fairly across borders further adds to the complexity.

Visionary Pathways and Catalysts for Change

1. United Nations Sustainable Development Goals (SDGs)
   The SDGs are a comprehensive framework for global economic reform, encompassing poverty eradication, environmental sustainability, gender equality, and more. These goals serve as a common compass, guiding nations toward a shared vision of unity and equity. Progress towards the SDGs relies on collaboration, innovation, and a collective commitment to transformative change.

2. Climate Action as a Driver of Reform
   The pressing necessity to combat climate change offers a persuasive drive for worldwide economic restructuring. Shifting towards sustainable energy sources, embracing circular economies, and curbing environmental deterioration necessitate comprehensive transformations that resonate with the values of unity and fairness. Green economic policies can stimulate growth while safeguarding the planet for future generations.

3. Innovative Financing Mechanisms
   Innovative financing mechanisms, such as global taxes on wealth or carbon emissions, can catalyze redistributive policies and equitable development. These mechanisms have the potential to generate resources that can be channeled towards uplifting marginalized communities, funding social programs, and advancing sustainable development projects.

The call for global economic reform reverberates as a clarion call, summoning nations, institutions, and individuals to embark on a transformative journey from disparities to unity. This journey is not one of convenience but necessity, driven by the imperatives of justice, sustainability, and shared prosperity. The blueprint for unity, rooted in redefined notions of growth, inclusive policies, responsible business practices, global cooperation, and the empowerment of the marginalized, offers a roadmap toward a more equitable and harmonious world. As challenges are confronted, and visionary pathways are traversed, the realization of this blueprint holds the promise of an economic landscape where disparities are bridged, unity prevails, and the symphony of human progress reaches its crescendo.

CHAPTER THREE

ECONOMIC EQUALITY THROUGH INCLUSIVE MULTILATERAL ARCHITECTURES

In an era defined by the rich tapestry of cultures, languages, and geographical variations that span the globe, the imperative to cultivate economic equality among nations emerges as a cardinal pursuit. In this intricate mosaic of humanity's interconnected aspirations for progress and well-being, the realization of a global harmony hinges upon establishing a balanced economic terrain that reveres the autonomy of each nation. This expanse of discourse intricately explores the foundational principles and intricate mechanisms imperative for constructing a groundbreaking paradigm of economic collaboration. This epoch orchestrates parity and fairness in the treatment of nations within multilateral agreements and trade accords.

At the heart of this transformative evolution lies the unwavering commitment to upholding the dignity of local currencies, fostering an environment where they stand as stalwart pillars of financial integrity and self-reliance. Moreover, this discourse distinctly underscores the monumental significance of responsible resource governance, casting it as an overarching tenet that steers the course of this novel economic narrative.

In this narrative, the stitches of inclusivity and equitable representation are meticulously woven, encapsulating the essence of unity amidst diversity. The chapters of this discourse traverse the corridors of policy, diplomacy, and collaborative action, unraveling the blueprints of multilateral architectures that transcend mere agreements, metamorphosing into living testaments of cooperation. By advocating for equal participation, irrespective of a nation's size or economic prowess, and by safeguarding the prerogatives of every currency within the global monetary spectrum, a symphony of economic concord begins to resonate.

As this journey unfolds, the narrative illuminates the paramountcy of stewarding resources responsibly – a collective responsibility that binds nations together in their shared commitment to sustainability and preservation. Thus, the narrative reframes the trajectory of economic engagement, navigating it toward an uncharted zenith of inclusivity, fairness, and shared prosperity.

TREATING NATIONS AS EQUALS

The journey towards achieving economic equality unfurls with a foundational dedication to viewing each nation as a coequal participant upon the global platform. It signifies a pledge to transcend the limitations of borders and boundaries, recognizing that the shared aspirations of nations are intricately interwoven. This commitment resonates beyond mere rhetoric; it embodies the essence of justice and progress, fostering an environment where no nation is relegated to a subservient position due to its economic size, historical journey, or geopolitical influence.

In the arena of multilateral and trade agreements, fairness stands as the keystone. It's a call to action that urges the architects of these agreements to dismantle power imbalances and rewrite the narratives that have often sidelined the voices of less influential nations. The size of an economy, the trajectory of history, and the global sway a nation wields should not serve as metrics to stifle its agency. Instead, these agreements should be a testament to the principles of collaboration and shared destiny.

However, the road toward economic equality isn't just about symbolic gestures; it's about fostering a tangible transformation. It requires constructing agreements that transcend mere transactional dynamics. They should cultivate an ecosystem where the gains aren't concentrated in a select few but where prosperity radiates through a network of balanced growth. These agreements should stand as blueprints for mutual benefit, promoting a reciprocal exchange of resources, knowledge, and advancements. The concept of equitable distribution takes center stage—nations rising together, bridging gaps, and ensuring that no corner of the global tapestry remains neglected or overlooked.

In this vision of economic equity, the journey isn't about a zero-sum game; it's about elevating the collective human experience. It's about fostering an environment where growth isn't a privilege reserved for a privileged few but a tide that lifts all boats. The commitment to treating nations as equals within the framework of multilateral and trade agreements is more than a sentiment—it's a profound shift that paves the way for a world where prosperity isn't confined to a select sphere but becomes the common heritage of humanity.

Foundation of Fairness

Multilateral agreements are the cornerstone of the intricate web of global economic interactions. They are not mere contractual documents but the tapestry of treaties, accords, and covenants that thread together the destinies of nations, economies, and dreams. Yet, as this intricate tapestry has unfolded over time, it has often been tainted by distortions—power dynamics, influence imbalances, and the unequal ability to shape the contours of engagement. This embedded inequality has occasionally pushed certain nations to the periphery of decision-making processes, corroding their inherent dignity and diminishing their agency.

Embarking on the transformative path toward economic equality necessitates a profound reimagining. It requires a redefinition that alters the very essence of multilateral agreements, infusing them with a potent blend of fairness, justice, and cooperation. In this envisioned landscape, a nation's economic size, historical trajectory, or global clout no longer serves as the yardstick for the volume of its voice or the scope of its rights. Every nation, irrespective of its global stature, has an identical seat at the negotiation table. This seat holds the promise of impartial representation and the authority to co-shape the destiny of collectives.

This recalibration is not merely symbolic; it's a declaration of intent. It signals a departure from conventional norms and paves the way for a world where partnership and participation transcend archaic hierarchies. Each nation's story is deemed invaluable, each perspective significant. Fairness isn't confined to diplomacy; it permeates the essence of international relations, kindling the flames of collaboration, camaraderie, and a shared commitment to realizing economic equity for all.

The Essence of Equitable Agreements

The transformational shift from self-interest to mutual benefit encapsulates a paradigm that traverses the terrain of pragmatism rather than dwelling in idealism alone. It finds its roots in the profound understanding that a myopic fixation on self-interest erodes the very fabric of shared humanity. Instead, this shift champions the concept of mutual benefit—a notion that resounds with the harmonious symphony of prosperity, where one nation's advancement need not be secured at the cost of another's well-being. It's an assertion that resonates with the interconnectedness of fates, emphasizing that the destinies of nations are intricately woven into an interdependent tapestry.

In the realm of international trade, this recalibration carries potent implications. It heralds the departure from a history laden with exploitative practices that have, through time, marginalized certain nations. In its stead, it beckons towards an avenue illuminated by balanced growth and symbiotic exchange. The significance of this shift extends beyond contractual formalities; it echoes in the harmonious resonance of interconnected economies, where each strand contributes to the resilience of the whole.

These equitable trade agreements aren't static legal documents; they pulsate with life, reflecting the interwoven nature of global economies. They carry a profound understanding that the gains harvested from such agreements should be channeled in a manner that elevates the weakest links, fostering an upward spiral of progress that elevates and uplifts all corners of the global tapestry.

Equity in Distribution: Beyond Accumulation to Inclusion

The principle of equitable distribution stands as a cornerstone in the transformative journey toward treating nations as equals. It serves as a counterpoint to the prevailing notion of economic growth—often characterized by aggregating wealth within a privileged subset of society. Instead, this principle heralds a profound shift in perspective, advocating for an economic landscape where the prosperity cultivated is not confined to the privileged elite but diffused across the societal spectrum.

The essence of equitable distribution resonates far beyond economic confines, reaching into the intricate fabric of socio-cultural dynamics. It is a clarion call that economic disparities cannot be considered in isolation, for they often intersect with and amplify existing social inequalities. In this symbiotic relationship, economic marginalization begets social marginalization, perpetuating a cycle of exclusion and furthering the divide between the haves and the have-nots.

The transformative power of equitable distribution lies in its capacity to break these chains of disparity. Through the adoption of this concept, societies strive to deconstruct the mechanisms that sustain cycles of marginalization. It demands a redistribution of resources and opportunities, ensuring that the benefits reaped from economic progress transcend socio-economic lines. No longer should prosperity be a privilege afforded only to a select few; instead, it should be a shared heritage that uplifts every stratum of society, regardless of their starting point.

This holistic perspective acknowledges that economic growth divorced from equity can fuel discontent and social unrest. When wealth is concentrated within privileged enclaves, it fosters discontentment among those who are denied entry to the abundance. This resentment can manifest in social unrest, political instability, and a general erosion of social cohesion. Inclusionary growth, on the other hand, offers a solution—an avenue for societies to mitigate tensions and foster a sense of collective prosperity.

The principle of equitable distribution carries profound implications for policy-making and societal frameworks. It underscores the need for targeted interventions that bridge gaps and uplift marginalized communities. These interventions go beyond mere handouts; they aim to provide equitable access to education, healthcare, and economic opportunities. By addressing the systemic barriers perpetuating inequality, societies can dismantle the structures that hinder progress for vast population segments.

At its heart, equitable distribution challenges the traditional dichotomy of winners and losers. It beckons a reframing of the narrative, shifting the focus from a zero-sum game to a collaborative endeavor. In this inclusive paradigm, nations no longer vie to amass the largest share of the pie; instead, they recognize that by expanding the pie and ensuring each slice is substantial, all can partake in the feast of progress.

However, implementing equitable distribution has its complexities. It necessitates a delicate balance, ensuring that incentives for innovation and entrepreneurship are preserved while safeguarding against the concentration of wealth. Mechanisms such as progressive taxation, social safety nets, and targeted investment in underserved areas become integral to this delicate equilibrium.

In practice, equitable distribution mandates a reevaluation of economic systems and the cultivation of a new mindset. It invites nations to recalibrate their priorities—transcending the narrow pursuit of economic growth for growth's sake and embracing a more inclusive vision of prosperity. This recalibration involves forging partnerships between governments, private enterprises, and civil society to build an ecosystem that nurtures inclusion.

The spirit of equitable distribution is grounded in a fundamental truth—economic prosperity can only be truly sustainable and meaningful when all share it. It embodies a vision where wealth catalyzes societal well-being, privilege is replaced with opportunity, and where the upliftment of the marginalized becomes a collective endeavor.

The principle of equitable distribution serves as a guiding star on the transformative journey toward treating nations as equals. It challenges the conventional narrative of economic accumulation, advocating for the diffusion of prosperity and the narrowing of disparities. By extending beyond economic realms and intertwining with socio-cultural dynamics, it strives to break the cycles of marginalization and exclusion. This principle redefines the concept of growth, urging societies to embrace inclusive progress that transcends the boundaries of privilege and ushers in an era where every individual, irrespective of their background, can share in the fruits of prosperity.

The Complexity of Equity: Challenges and Contemplations

Embarking on the journey towards treating nations as equals comes with a tapestry of challenges, each woven into the fabric of history, power dynamics, and intricate interconnections. It necessitates a recalibration of the foundations of power structures that have upheld inequality for generations. This demands a profound shift in how influence is wielded, decisions are made, and the acknowledgment that no nation's voice should carry more weight than another's on the global stage.

The journey toward equality also involves untangling the threads of historical injustices that continue to cast shadows over the present. Acknowledging and addressing these historical wrongs is an act of justice and a step toward healing. This involves grappling with complex narratives, recognizing the trauma inflicted by centuries of colonialism, exploitation, and marginalization. It's an acknowledgment that economic inequality is often rooted in historical imbalances, and rectifying this necessitates addressing historical wounds.

Navigating the complex webs of interdependence is another challenge that cannot be underestimated. In a globalized world, nations are intricately linked through trade, politics, and shared resources. Pursuing economic equality demands a delicate balancing act, where collaboration is prioritized over competition. It requires nations to rise above narrow interests and envision a collective tapestry of progress that benefits all.

This transformative journey requires an unwavering commitment to justice, even in the face of resistance. The forces that uphold inequality are deeply entrenched, and breaking free from their grasp requires unyielding determination. This means confronting entrenched interests and questioning the status quo. It means recognizing that genuine progress might face opposition from those who benefit from the current disparities.

Delving deeper, this journey invites introspection into the mechanisms through which privilege and advantage are perpetuated. It explores the unearned advantages that certain nations possess and the systems that sustain them. Unpacking these mechanisms requires a reckoning with uncomfortable truths and an honest examination of how systemic biases have been perpetuated over time.

Furthermore, this journey beckons for a surge of creativity and innovation. The path to economic equality is not a well-trodden road but a labyrinthine maze that demands new perspectives and innovative solutions. This requires thinking beyond traditional models and embracing novel approaches that challenge existing norms. It means designing economic systems that are not just equitable on the surface, but that actively counteract the structural inequalities that have endured for centuries.

Constructing frameworks ensuring accountability, transparency, and participation becomes paramount. As nations collaborate to redefine their relationships, transparency becomes a cornerstone, ensuring that power is not wielded in secret corridors. Accountability becomes a means to hold all parties responsible for their commitments, creating a culture of trust that underpins cooperation.

Above all, this transformative journey calls for the cultivation of global citizens. It's a collective endeavor to nurture individuals who recognize that they are part of a larger whole and that their choices and actions ripple across borders. This journey demands the fostering of empathy that transcends national boundaries, realizing that pursuing economic equality is not just a national endeavor but a shared global aspiration.

The complexity of the journey towards treating nations as equals is an intricate tapestry woven with challenges and contemplations. It requires navigating historical injustices, recalibrating power dynamics, and fostering innovation. It demands a steadfast commitment to justice, transparency, and accountability. Above all, it necessitates a fundamental shift in how we perceive ourselves—as citizens of nations and inhabitants of a shared planet. This journey is not just about reshaping economies; it's about reshaping our collective destiny.

A Vision Unveiled: Beyond Rhetoric to Action

The transformational journey towards treating nations as equals goes beyond mere rhetoric; it demands concrete action, active engagement, and collaborative efforts. This call reverberates across nations, beckoning governments, international organizations, civil society, and individuals to join hands in a unified pursuit - dismantling the entrenched barriers perpetuating inequality.

An integral facet of this transformative odyssey is the empowerment of marginalized nations. History bears witness to certain regions grappling with deep-rooted biases that have relegated them to the periphery of economic advancement. Treating nations as equals necessitates a concentrated endeavor to uplift these marginalized entities. This commitment mandates targeted interventions addressing the bedrock causes of their marginalization, be they historical legacies, structural imbalances, or systemic injustices. Each nation attains an equitable stake in shaping global discourse by fostering a narrative shift.

Diplomacy becomes a transformative instrument, transcending its role from mere negotiation to collaborative partnership. It evolves beyond safeguarding national interests, ascending to a shared well-being. The art of diplomatic negotiation turns into a harmonious dance of shared aspirations, with compromise reflecting strength, not weakness. Diplomats cease to be mere representatives; they metamorphose into champions of shared humanity, advocating solutions that elevate the collective good.

The transformative journey extends into education, nurturing a global citizenry marked by empathy and understanding. Education evolves into a catalyst for change, breaking down the barriers of ignorance and prejudice. It becomes a conduit for comprehending the intricate interplay between historical trajectories and current realities, thus illuminating a path toward reconciliation and collaboration. This shift in education equips individuals to play a pivotal role in the collective pursuit of a just world.

The journey towards equal treatment mandates an overhaul of economic systems. It necessitates transcending the conventional pursuit of profit to embrace a holistic paradigm rooted in human dignity and planetary well-being. Economic policies shift from being solely profit-driven to advancing the collective welfare, ensuring that prosperity becomes a universal right, not a selective privilege. This recalibration aligns economic systems with the mission of creating an inclusive global economy.

Sustainability emerges as the guiding principle, intertwining economic equality with the imperative of preserving the planet's health and securing the legacy for future generations. As nations treat each other as equals, they embrace shared environmental responsibility. This shift demands moving away from exploitative practices and embracing regenerative strategies that nurture ecosystems and counteract the impacts of climate change.

In culmination, the journey towards treating nations as equals is a collective narrative, binding the destinies of nations and individuals beyond borders and ideologies. In an era poised at the crossroads of promise and challenge, the choice to embark on this transformative journey hinges upon a foundational truth – a nation's worth is not measured by its wealth or influence but by its dedication to upholding the principles of dignity and equality. In this collective commitment, a new world beckons – a world where the fabric of economic equity is woven with threads of cooperation, compassion, and unity.

EMPOWERING LOCAL CURRENCIES AND SETTLEMENTS

The principle of according to equal respect for currencies stands as a foundational pillar of achieving economic equality on the global stage. However, in the current economic landscape, this principle is often overshadowed by the prevalence of a limited set of dominant currencies in international transactions. This dominance creates a skewed environment that introduces unwarranted risks and volatility, particularly for nations whose currencies are undervalued or less recognized.

A transformative shift is required to rectify this imbalance and usher in a new era of economic collaboration. This shift emphasizes conducting settlements in local currencies whenever feasible, representing a departure from the prevailing dependency on a handful of dominant currencies. By embracing this approach, nations can effectively reduce their vulnerability to the unpredictable fluctuations of these dominant currencies, which often result from factors beyond their control.

In addition to mitigating risk, empowering settlements in local currencies offers a profound opportunity for nations to harness the inherent value of their monetary systems. This shift in perspective marks a departure from the conventional norm, where the focus primarily revolves around the dominant currencies. Empowering local currencies allows nations to exert greater control over their economic destiny, fostering a sense of sovereignty and self-determination. In this process, countries can lay the foundation for a more equitable and harmonious economic structure, where the merits and capacities of each currency are acknowledged and appreciated on a global level.

The Global Imbalance: Dominant Currencies and Systemic Risks

In today's global economy, the significance of currencies in facilitating cross-border trade and financial transactions cannot be overstated. Over time, specific currencies have become prominent, assuming the role of dominant players in the international arena. The United States Dollar, Euro, Japanese Yen, and British Pound have occupied prominent positions in this league, facilitating worldwide transactions and trade accords. However, while these currencies have undoubtedly eased international commerce's wheels, they have inadvertently contributed to a lopsided system characterized by systemic risks and vulnerabilities.

The prevailing reliance on a limited array of dominant currencies lays bare the fragility of the global financial system. The values of these currencies are subject to fluctuations triggered by diverse factors – economic shifts, political decisions, speculative activities, and more. The far-reaching consequences of such fluctuations resonate across borders, creating ripple effects that reverberate through economies worldwide. For nations with undervalued or less recognized currencies, this scenario places them in a precarious position. Their economies become disproportionately exposed to the volatility associated with the movements of these dominant currencies.

This exposure, in turn, can trigger a range of detrimental outcomes. Trade imbalances may arise as the exchange rates influenced by these dominant currencies skew the terms of international trade in favor of nations whose currencies are stronger. Additionally, the unpredictability introduced by currency volatility can result in capital flight from nations with weaker currencies, undermining their economic stability and prospects for growth. The challenges faced by these nations are further compounded, hampering their quest for equitable economic progress and development.

To illustrate this phenomenon, let's consider the case of a developing nation whose currency is undervalued compared to dominant counterparts like the US Dollar or Euro. Despite the nation's efforts to bolster its economy, the fluctuations in the value of these dominant currencies can render its exports less competitive in the global market. As a result, trade imbalances may arise, hampering the nation's ability to achieve balanced growth and participate fully in the global trade network.

The recent history of the Eurozone offers another pertinent example. The Euro, a dominant currency backed by multiple economies, faced significant challenges during the European debt crisis. The shared currency's value was affected by the economic struggles of certain member countries, leading to systemic risks that affected the entire Eurozone and even reverberated globally. This event underscored the vulnerability that can arise from overreliance on a few dominant currencies, exposing economies to external shocks and disruptions.

In light of these considerations, a paradigm shift is necessary to foster economic equality among nations. This shift calls for a departure from the status quo of relying solely on a handful of dominant currencies for international transactions. Instead, empowering local currencies in settlement mechanisms can lead to a more equitable and stable economic landscape. By settling transactions in local currencies, nations can reduce their exposure to the volatility of dominant currencies and gain greater control over their economic destinies. This approach mitigates risks and empowers nations to harness the value of their monetary systems, fostering a more inclusive and balanced global economic order.

The current state of dominant currencies in the global financial system carries both advantages and inherent risks. The overreliance on a limited number of currencies creates a fragile economic environment where value fluctuations can trigger far-reaching consequences. Developing nations with undervalued currencies are especially vulnerable to these dynamics, facing trade imbalances and economic instability. However, nations can mitigate risks and empower themselves to pursue more equitable economic growth by shifting towards settling transactions in local currencies. This transformation marks a pivotal step towards fostering economic equality among nations and promoting a stable and inclusive global economy.

Redefining Settlements in Local Currencies

A transformative approach is needed to rectify this imbalance and forge a path toward economic equality. This approach centers on the empowerment of local currencies and settlements – a shift that holds the potential to reshape the dynamics of international trade and finance.

At this paradigm shift's core lies the currency respect and equal treatment principle. Regardless of their economic might, nations deserve the opportunity to engage in transactions on an equitable footing. This entails recognizing the intrinsic value of each nation's currency and conducting settlements in local currencies whenever feasible. By doing so, the dependence on a select few dominant currencies is alleviated, reducing vulnerability to their fluctuations and mitigating systemic risks.

Empowering local currencies and settlements is a multidimensional endeavor that requires collaboration among nations, financial institutions, and international organizations. Establishing mechanisms that facilitate transactions in local currencies can catalyze economic empowerment. Bilateral and multilateral agreements encouraging local currencies can lead to increased stability and predictability in international trade. Furthermore, implementing innovative financial technologies can streamline the currency conversion process, making settlements in local currencies a viable and efficient option for businesses and governments alike.

Fostering Sovereignty and Economic Resilience

The empowerment of local currencies and promotion of settlements in those currencies encompass more than just economic advantages; they signify a profound assertion of sovereignty and self-determination. When nations opt to conduct transactions using their currencies, they reclaim significant control over their economic trajectory. This autonomy becomes particularly pivotal for nations grappling with undervalued currencies. By embracing local currencies and settlements, these nations can effectively break free from the cycle of reliance on dominant currencies, thereby asserting their rightful position on the global economic stage.

This approach goes beyond economic pragmatism; it becomes a strategic move to secure and strengthen national identity. By transacting in their currencies, nations reaffirm their individuality and enhance their economic self-sufficiency. This transformation nurtures a feeling of proprietorship concerning economic policies and choices, empowering nations to customize their strategies to align with their distinct requirements and ambitions. The empowerment derived from local currencies fosters renewed self-confidence, enabling nations to engage in international trade and finance on their terms.

Furthermore, the embrace of local currencies and settlements bolsters economic resilience – a critical attribute in an interconnected and unpredictable world. These measures function as a buffer against external shocks and disruptions that often emanate from the volatility of dominant currencies. When transactions occur in local currencies, nations create a shield against the cascading impacts of currency fluctuations. This protective layer is a safeguard for national economies, ensuring they are not unduly exposed to the risks and uncertainties tied to the value swings of dominant currencies.

A prime example of this concept can be observed in countries that have opted to promote using their local currencies in trade agreements. China's efforts to internationalize the Chinese Yuan (Renminbi) exemplify how a deliberate shift toward local currencies can enhance economic resilience. By encouraging trade partners to settle transactions in Yuan, China not only reduces its exposure to external currency risks but also reinforces the stability of its financial system. This approach positions China as a stronger player in the global economy, with a currency that holds greater influence and stability.

In the wake of the aftermath of the 2008 global financial crisis, the vulnerability of nations relying solely on predominant currencies was starkly emphasized. Countries found themselves at the mercy of external economic forces as the fluctuation of dominant currencies sent shockwaves through their economies. Those with local currency-based systems were better equipped to weather the storm, their economic foundations more stable and less susceptible to external turbulence.

The empowerment of local currencies and settlements extends beyond economic advantages; it resonates deeply with sovereignty, self-determination, and economic resilience principles. Nations that opt to transact in their currencies seize the opportunity to exercise greater control over their economic destinies, freeing themselves from dependency on dominant currencies. This move enhances their economic self-sufficiency and fortifies their identities and standing in the global economic realm. Moreover, local currencies serve as a shield against the volatility of dominant currencies, bolstering economic resilience and insulating nations from external shocks. As the world navigates an ever-evolving economic landscape, embracing local currencies and settlements emerges as a prudent strategy for nations to secure their economic well-being and assert their autonomy.

The Path Ahead: Challenges and Opportunities

The journey towards empowering local currencies and settlements is full of challenges. It necessitates a fundamental shift in perspective, where nations collectively acknowledge the significance of each currency and commit to impartial treatment. Additionally, the establishment of the necessary infrastructure, including efficient currency conversion mechanisms and supportive regulatory frameworks, demands collaborative efforts on a global scale.

However, within these challenges lie remarkable opportunities. Empowering local currencies can create a more inclusive and resilient global financial system. It can foster closer economic ties among nations, engendering trust and cooperation. Moreover, it can spark innovation in financial technology, driving the development of solutions that facilitate seamless cross-border transactions in local currencies.

The transformational journey towards empowering local currencies and settlements is essential to realizing economic equality among nations. It is a journey that requires a reimagining of the international economic order, one that values the sovereignty of nations and respects the diversity of currencies. By shifting the focus from dominant currencies to local currencies, nations can free themselves from dependency, embrace their economic potential, and forge a future marked by cooperation, resilience, and prosperity. As the world navigates through the complexities of the modern economic landscape, the call for empowering local currencies and settlements resonates as a powerful and resonant symbol of a just and equitable global order.

RESPONSIBLE RESOURCE MANAGEMENT

Within the complex web of global interactions, resource exploitation emerges as a pervasive concern, casting a prolonged darkness that fuels a cycle of inequity reverberating through nations and epochs. The call for economic equality rings hollow if it does not encompass responsible resource management – a fundamental pillar on which a just and equitable global order can be built. This imperative stems from a realization that true economic parity cannot be achieved until every nation exercises sovereign control over its resources, shielded from the specter of exploitation that has marred history.

Resource exploitation has often unfolded as a tale of the powerful exploiting the vulnerable, a narrative woven into the annals of colonialism and economic imperialism. The asymmetry of power in the global arena has frequently translated into an unbalanced distribution of resources. The consequences are not merely economic; they resonate across ecological, social, and geopolitical dimensions, creating fractures in the very fabric of human civilization.

The paradigm must shift from plunder to stewardship to forge a path toward economic equality. This transformation calls for promoting sustainable resource management practices that prioritize the preservation of ecosystems, biodiversity, and the planet's overall health. It demands that nations, regardless of their economic stature, adopt responsible extraction methods that minimize environmental degradation and prioritize regeneration. This shift toward sustainability is not just an ethical imperative, but also a strategic necessity, for the health of economies is intimately intertwined with the health of the environment.

Responsible resource management goes beyond ecological contemplations. It encompasses establishing equitable partnerships that guarantee the impartial and equitable distribution of benefits derived from these resources. Historically, resource-rich nations have often been left grappling with the paradox of plenty – abundant resources coupled with disproportionate poverty. This paradox underscores the urgent need for international agreements that guarantee that the wealth generated from resource extraction is shared with local communities, empowering them and contributing to their economic advancement.

A poignant example of responsible resource management can be found in Norway's approach to its oil reserves. While endowed with vast oil wealth, Norway recognized the potential pitfalls of reckless exploitation. Instead of squandering this resource, Norway established a sovereign wealth fund that invests a significant portion of oil revenues for future generations. This forward-thinking strategy embodies the essence of economic equality, as it safeguards the interests of both the present and the future, ensuring that the benefits of resources are not ephemeral but enduring.

Furthermore, the concept of responsible resource management extends to a global perspective. The interdependence of nations in an increasingly interconnected world necessitates collaborative efforts to conserve resources for the collective good. Climate change, driven in part by resource-intensive activities, is a glaring reminder of the urgent need for responsible resource management on a global scale. The Paris Agreement, a landmark accord adopted by nearly all nations, exemplifies a collective commitment to mitigating the impact of resource-intensive practices. It stands as evidence of the understanding that the conscientious utilization of resources surpasses boundaries and ideologies, uniting nations in a collective endeavor to preserve the planet for present and forthcoming generations.

The pursuit of economic equality is intrinsically linked to responsible resource management. It requires a profound shift in mindset – from exploitation to stewardship, from short-term gains to long-term sustainability. It demands that nations assume the mantle of guardians of their resources, adopting practices that ensure ecological integrity, social equity, and international cooperation. Responsible resource management is not merely a technical matter; it is a moral imperative that reflects a commitment to forging a just and equitable world. Amid the challenges encountered by the global community in the 21st century, the conscientious management of resources emerges as a critical stride towards attaining economic parity, nurturing worldwide stability, and safeguarding the vibrancy of our planet for the generations that follow.

Inclusivity of Reserve Currencies

When it comes to global finance, the notion of reserve currencies has long held sway over international economic dynamics. However, as the world becomes increasingly interconnected, the existing framework for determining reserve currency status reveals a chink in its armor, one that perpetuates economic disparities among nations. A radical shift toward economic equality beckons, underpinned by a novel approach: the inclusivity of reserve currencies.

Historically, a few dominant currencies have held sway as reserve currencies, wielding significant sway over the global financial framework. The United States Dollar, Euro, Japanese Yen, and the British Pound have been pillars of international trade and finance, profoundly shaping economic transactions. Yet, this concentration of reserve currencies inadvertently propels a cycle of inequality, where nations whose currencies are overlooked or undervalued find themselves marginalized within the economic arena.

A transformative step toward rectifying this imbalance is the recalibration of reserve currency criteria. By adopting a benchmark linked to GDP size – a pragmatic measure like 1 trillion or 2 trillion USD – the landscape of reserve currencies undergoes a paradigm shift. This strategic pivot doesn't just usher in financial diversity; it fosters a level playing field by allowing a broader spectrum of currencies to contribute to global economic stability. Such an approach serves as an antidote to the vulnerabilities inherent in a system dominated by a few currencies, curtailing the ripple effects of economic turbulence that disproportionately impact nations tethered to these dominant currencies.

The inclusivity of reserve currencies is more than a conceptual overhaul; it's a tangible catalyst for economic growth. This revised criterion extends an invitation to nations to accelerate their economic trajectories, vying for a coveted spot among the reserve currencies. Emerging and developed nations are nudged toward fostering growth and innovation, knowing that their efforts could lead to international recognition and economic elevation. This dynamic spurs a positive feedback loop wherein nations are incentivized to enhance their economic prowess, thus contributing to a more balanced global economic architecture.

A glance at history reveals the profound impact of currency inclusivity. A pertinent example is China's drive to internationalize the yuan (renminbi). China's strategic efforts to position the yuan as a global reserve currency have advanced its own economic interests and instigated a broader conversation about redefining the balance of economic power. The acknowledgment of the yuan in the International Monetary Fund's Special Drawing Rights basket represents a significant stride toward inclusivity, validating the potency of revisiting reserve currency norms.

Moreover, the inclusivity of reserve currencies magnifies the democratization of financial systems. Smaller nations, often overlooked within the traditional reserve currency framework, are now presented with a platform to demonstrate their economic mettle. This empowerment echoes through local economies, fueling innovation, employment, and sustainable development. It signals a shift from a top-heavy financial paradigm to a decentralized one, where multiple currencies collaboratively contribute to global financial resilience.

The inclusivity of reserve currencies epitomizes a transformative leap toward economic equality. It challenges the status quo, offering a remedy to the concentration of power and influence within the hands of a few dominant currencies. This recalibration isn't merely a theoretical endeavor; it's a blueprint for fostering a more balanced and equitable global economic order. As nations stand at the crossroads of economic evolution, the embrace of currency inclusivity beckons, heralding a future where diversity, growth, and prosperity are intertwined in a tapestry of mutual benefit.

Sustainable Growth and Development

At the heart of the global stage, a profound challenge echoes across nations and reverberates through time: the issue of resource exploitation. This challenge, deeply embedded within the fabric of international interactions, has given rise to a cycle of inequality that casts a prolonged shadow, perpetuating disparities and echoing through the corridors of history.

Resource exploitation, driven by economic interests and power dynamics, has historically led to the depletion of resources from less powerful nations to benefit more powerful ones. This phenomenon spans various domains, from extracting natural resources to trade imbalances and appropriating cultural heritage. The consequences of this exploitation are far-reaching, leaving marginalized nations at a disadvantage, both economically and socially.

The consequences of resource exploitation are not confined to economic disparities alone; they also extend to social and environmental dimensions. Exploitative practices often exacerbate existing social inequalities, contributing to the marginalization of vulnerable communities within a nation. Additionally, the reckless extraction of resources can lead to irreversible environmental damage, impacting ecosystems and contributing to climate change. As a result, the pursuit of economic equality demands an urgent reevaluation of resource management practices.

In this pursuit, the concept of responsible resource management emerges as a guiding principle. Responsible resource management encompasses a range of strategies and practices to ensure the sustainable use of resources while considering the long-term interests of both nations and the global community. It involves a shift away from short-sighted exploitation towards a holistic approach that integrates economic, social, and environmental considerations.

The sustainable development goals function as a roadmap for conscientious resource management. These objectives, formulated by the United Nations, underscore the necessity of harmonizing economic advancement with social inclusivity and environmental preservation. Through the embrace of sustainable practices, nations can secure their resources for future generations while concurrently fostering economic expansion and diminishing inequality.

Consider the example of mineral extraction. Instead of allowing multinational corporations to exploit resources without oversight, responsible resource management involves implementing regulations that ensure fair compensation, minimal environmental impact, and the equitable distribution of benefits within the nation. This approach protects the interests of the local population and contributes to a more just global economic landscape.

Furthermore, responsible resource management necessitates collaboration on a global scale. International agreements and frameworks play a crucial role in regulating the exploitation of resources that transcend national boundaries. For instance, agreements related to the management of marine resources in international waters or the protection of biodiversity through conventions like the Convention on Biological Diversity are integral to ensuring responsible resource management on a global level.

Implementing responsible resource management requires a multi-pronged approach. Firstly, nations must enact comprehensive regulatory frameworks that address environmental, social, and economic concerns. These regulations should incentivize sustainable practices, penalize irresponsible behavior, and ensure that benefits are equitably distributed. Secondly, transparent monitoring and reporting mechanisms should be established to hold both nations and corporations accountable for their resource management practices.

Moreover, the transition to responsible resource management involves technological innovation and capacity building. Advancements in sustainable technologies can reduce the environmental impact of resource extraction and processing. Additionally, providing technical assistance and knowledge sharing to nations with limited resources can empower them to adopt responsible practices that align with their economic and developmental goals.

A compelling example of responsible resource management can be found in Norway's approach to oil and gas extraction. As a major oil producer, Norway has implemented stringent regulations to ensure environmental sustainability and fair revenue distribution. The government has established a sovereign wealth fund that invests a portion of oil revenues to benefit future generations. This approach supports economic equality within Norway and showcases how responsible resource management can be a model for others to follow.

The issue of resource exploitation has deep-seated implications for economic equality, environmental sustainability, and social justice. Responsible resource management stands as a beacon of hope in addressing these challenges, forging a path toward a more equitable and harmonious global landscape. By embracing sustainable practices, enacting comprehensive regulations, and fostering international collaboration, nations can pave the way for a future where resources are managed responsibly and the cycle of inequality is broken. The journey towards responsible resource management is not just an obligation; it's a shared commitment to a better world for present and future generations alike.

CHAPTER FOUR

EQUAL RIGHTS OF NATIONS

The principle of Equal Rights of Nations conveys the core notion that every country, irrespective of its size, influence, or geopolitical status, merits equivalent respect and entitlements within the global community.

It recognizes each nation's inherent dignity and sovereignty, emphasizing that no nation should be subjugated or marginalized due to economic, political, or social disparities. This concept affirms that each nation is entitled to engage in global matters with parity. These shape determinations impact its future and receive just and equitable treatment from other nations.

At its core, the equal rights of nations underscore the need for a balanced and just world order where power imbalances are eradicated and cooperation prevails over exploitation. This principle extends beyond diplomacy and politics; it permeates economic interactions, trade agreements, environmental protection, and the pursuit of global peace. It is a call to dismantle systemic inequalities that have historically favored certain nations while disadvantaging others. The equal rights of nations serve as a cornerstone for building a world where unity, diversity, and shared prosperity prevail.

In international relations, each nation contributes a unique note, a distinct melody that shapes the grand composition of global harmony. Yet, not all voices have been granted equal resonance. For too long, the world stage has been dominated by the powerful, their voices amplified while the whispers of the marginalized remain unheard. Amidst this discord, the concept of "Equal Rights of Nations" emerges, seeking to restore equilibrium to the symphony of sovereignty.

Imagine a world where the size of a nation's landmass holds no sway over the magnitude of its influence. Imagine a community where economic prowess is balanced with the intrinsic value of cultural heritage and human dignity. This is the world envisioned by the equal rights of nations – a world where the chorus of voices, whether from sprawling continents or tiny archipelagos, resounds with the same weight and importance.

This chapter delves into the tapestry of equal rights that weaves nations together, transcending boundaries and ideologies. We explore how the principle of equal rights challenges the status quo, disrupting the patterns of dominance that have shaped history. Through the lens of diplomacy, trade, resource management, and sustainable development, we uncover the profound impact that recognizing and upholding the equal rights of nations can have on the global stage.

THE FUNDAMENTAL PRINCIPLE OF EQUAL RIGHTS AMONG NATIONS

In the global landscape, where diverse cultures interlace, economies merge, and common aspirations give birth to a symphony of unity, a fundamental principle emerges, much like the North Star guiding nations towards a harmonious coexistence. This principle, akin to an eternal melody echoing beyond borders, unveils the anthem of equal rights among nations. It's a pledge that each nation, irrespective of its stature, possesses an unassailable right to waltz to the tune of self-determination, to compose its narrative on the canvas of sovereignty, and to stand united on the worldwide stage of collective aspirations.

At its core, this principle recognizes that the sovereignty of nations is an intrinsic facet entwined with the threads of self-governance and cultural identity. It is the bedrock on which international relationships are forged, underpinning diplomacy, trade, and shared endeavors. The principle's essence resonates in the halls of the United Nations, where diverse voices converge to discuss, negotiate, and aspire to create a world where the sanctity of equality overshadows the concept of might. Through the lens of history and jurisprudence, it is evident that equal rights among nations are not merely a concept but a palpable reality. This framework shapes the destiny of humanity.

Historical and Legal Foundations

The principle of equal rights among nations is a testament to the progressing story of human civilization, interwoven across historical epochs and united by the intricate fabric of legality. Its roots can be retraced to pivotal junctures that have molded the contemporary world.

The emergence of the Westphalian Treaty in 1648 marked a turning point in the evolution of nation-states. This landmark agreement, which concluded the Thirty Years' War, introduced the concept of state sovereignty and territorial integrity. The Treaty of Westphalia forged the notion that nations had the right to chart their destinies, free from external interference. This embryonic seedling of equal rights laid the foundation for the principle that would later blossom into a vital doctrine in international relations.

Fast forward to 1945, the aftermath of a world ravaged by two devastating World Wars and on the cusp of a new era witnessed the establishment of the United Nations (UN). A unified reaction to the atrocities of conflict, the UN Charter infused vitality into the principle of equal rights among nations. At its essence, the Charter entrenched the principles of sovereign equality and the prohibition of meddling in the internal affairs of states. This pivotal moment of global solidarity marked a conscious step towards acknowledging the inherent rights of all nations, irrespective of their size, economic prowess, or political influence.

As the convocation of diverse nations, the United Nations was envisioned as a beacon of hope, a platform for dialogue, cooperation, and shared aspirations. The Charter's fundamental commitment to equal rights among nations was a clarion call to transcend the old paradigms of power politics and forge a new trajectory that honored the sanctity of sovereignty.

The journey of equal rights found expression in grand charters and the multitude of international treaties and customary laws that evolved over time. These documents, signed and ratified by nations, underscored the enduring commitment to equal rights, ensuring that this principle became an inseparable part of the global legal fabric. From the Geneva Conventions to the Universal Declaration of Human Rights, from the Vienna Convention on Diplomatic Relations to the Rome Statute of the Within the framework of the International Criminal Court, the principle of equal rights among nations resounds as a fundamental pillar that sustains the very core of these agreements.

The historical and legal foundations of equal rights among nations are deeply intertwined, spanning centuries and continents. From the seeds sown in the Westphalian Treaty to the blossoming of the United Nations and from crafting international treaties to establishing customary laws, the principle is firmly entrenched. It serves as a testament to humanity's collective endeavor to foster a world where nations, regardless of their disparities, are united by mutual respect, cooperation, and shared progress.

Sovereignty and Self-Determination

Sovereignty and self-determination are the bedrock principles of equal rights among nations. These principles, deeply interwoven into the fabric of global discourse, encapsulate the essence of a world where nations govern their destinies and aspirations flourish unencumbered.

Sovereignty, a concept rooted in the Westphalian Treaty and crystallized over centuries, is the guardian of a nation's autonomy. It signifies an unassailable right that every nation possesses the exclusive prerogative to shape its internal affairs without external intrusion. Within the realm of sovereignty lies the power to preserve cultural heritage, protect the rights of citizens, and exercise governance as a manifestation of national identity. In a world of diverse cultures and traditions, the principle of sovereignty provides the canvas on which nations can paint their distinctive narratives.

Conversely, self-determination amplifies the symphony of sovereignty by affording nations the liberty to forge their destinies. It is the right of nations to determine their political, economic, and cultural trajectories freely. Self-determination honors the authenticity of each nation's journey, recognizing that their progress need not mimic a predetermined model but should resonate with their unique context. This principle is vital for nurturing sustainable development, empowering marginalized communities, and forging pathways toward equitable prosperity.

Moreover, the harmonious interplay of sovereignty and self-determination contributes immeasurably to global stability. When nations are assured of their sovereignty, they become active participants in a collective narrative, fostering a sense of trust and collaboration.

By allowing nations to sculpt their own futures, self-determination minimizes the potential for resentment and alienation that can fuel conflicts.

By placing the reins of governance in the hands of nations, these principles cultivate an atmosphere of peaceful coexistence. The foundation for fruitful diplomacy and cooperation is established when each nation's distinct identity is valued and its aspirations respected. The absence of external imposition promotes diplomatic dialogue, fostering understanding and mitigating the risk of misunderstandings that can breed hostility.

In essence, sovereignty and self-determination are not merely theoretical concepts; they are the cornerstones of a world in which nations' external influences do not shackle nations' principles. They are the keys to a harmonious world where diverse voices harmonize and cooperation supersedes conflict. They beckon us towards a future where equal rights flourish, bridging gaps, celebrating diversity, and paving the way for a global tapestry woven with the threads of mutual respect and collective progress.

Non-Discrimination and Non-Intervention

Equal rights among nations entail the prohibition of discrimination and intervention by more powerful nations in the internal affairs of others. These principles stand as firm pillars, staunchly opposing the specter of prejudice and the shadow of undue interference that can disrupt the delicate equilibrium of international relations.

Non-discrimination, a beacon that has illuminated the path towards justice throughout history, extends its brilliance to the realm of nations. It's the solemn affirmation that every nation, regardless of size, wealth, or influence, merits equal treatment. This principle underlines the irrefutable truth that all nations share a common platform of respect and mutual recognition. By rejecting the toxic notion of hierarchy, non-discrimination fosters an environment where decisions are reached collaboratively and the interests of all are validated.

Parallel to non-discrimination, the principle of non-intervention stands as a guardian of national autonomy.

It is a firm declaration that powerful countries must refrain from interfering in other people's internal issues, respecting the sacred space each country deserves to develop its sovereign identity.

A symphony of impartiality resonates by championing non-intervention, silencing the dissonance of manipulation and coercion. This principle doesn›t merely shield weaker nations; it empowers them to chart their destinies and foster self-reliance.

Collective decision-making, a cornerstone of these principles, crystallizes the essence of diplomacy. Decisions shaped by the collaborative symphony of diverse nations are inherently more robust and representative in a world where every voice counts. Non-discrimination and non-intervention harmonize within the framework of shared decision-making, forging alliances that transcend the confines of self-interest and ushering in an era where diplomacy is an instrument of understanding rather than dominance.

The significance of non-discrimination and non-intervention cannot be overstated in their contribution to conflict prevention. These principles preclude the ignition of discord by extinguishing the sparks of inequality and repression. When nations are free from the specter of external interference, they're more inclined to focus on growth, development, and international cooperation, contributing to a tapestry woven with threads of mutual respect and shared progress.

Non-discrimination and non-intervention illuminate the path toward a world where nations coexist in an ecosystem of respect and mutual understanding. They carve a space where the symphony of diplomacy flourishes and where the empowerment of nations, irrespective of their might, fosters a fabric of unity. Upholding these principles, we not only safeguard the equal rights of nations but also nurture a legacy of equilibrium, harmony, and a world where the resplendent hues of diversity illuminate the stage of international relations.

International Cooperation and Collective Security

The principle of equal rights among nations resonates as an individualistic affirmation and a collective anthem of international cooperation. This principle envisions a world where nations collaborate harmoniously, pooling their strengths to address shared challenges, navigate complex issues, and champion the common good.

Collaborative initiatives serve as tangible manifestations of this principle. Trade agreements, for instance, weave economic ties that transcend borders, fostering prosperity through mutually beneficial exchanges. Climate accords acknowledge the universal responsibility to safeguard our planet, where nations collectively commit to mitigating environmental degradation. In humanitarian endeavors, nations band together to alleviate suffering in times of crisis, recognizing the interconnectedness of human well-being.

Collective security mechanisms are another profound manifestation of the principle of equal rights. Institutions like the United Nations establish frameworks that emphasize mutual defense and the prevention of conflicts. These mechanisms underscore the pivotal role of unity in safeguarding peace, emphasizing that a threat to one nation's security is a concern for all. The concept of "collective security" encapsulates the shared understanding that the safety of the global community hinges upon the collective resolve to prevent aggression and maintain stability.

However, the practical implementation of these ideals encounters the intricate tapestry of geopolitics, power dynamics, and cultural nuances. The challenge lies in harmonizing national interests with the pursuit of global welfare. Geopolitical ambitions can often eclipse the spirit of cooperation, hindering progress in initiatives like disarmament and environmental protection. The power dynamics inherent in international relations sometimes grant disproportionate influence to certain nations, undermining equal rights.

The United Nations Security Council exemplifies the potential and challenges in implementing equal rights among nations. While constructed with the intent of safeguarding international peace and security, the structure and veto authority of the Security Council has initiated dialogues regarding equity and inclusiveness. The principle of equal rights occasionally clashes with political realities, as influential nations exert their influence over decisions in manners that may not invariably harmonize with the broader global welfare.

The principle of equal rights among nations weaves a complex yet harmonious tapestry of international cooperation and collective security. It is a testament to the power of unity in addressing global challenges and securing peace. While challenges persist due to the intricacies of geopolitics and power dynamics, the ongoing pursuit of equal rights serves as a reminder that the symphony of cooperation and shared responsibility can harmonize the diverse voices of nations on the global stage.

Strategies to Promote Equal Rights Among Nations

Promoting equal rights among nations requires a multifaceted approach that embraces diplomacy, cooperation, and empowerment. Here are key guiding strategies to foster an environment where nations can thrive on the foundation of equality:

1. Promoting Diplomacy: Diplomacy is the linchpin for ensuring equal rights among nations. Nations can peacefully resolve disputes and work towards common goals by engaging in open dialogues and negotiations.

2. Enhancing International Organizations: By bolstering the capabilities and efficacy of international entities, such as the UN, the execution of equal rights principles can be improved through unbiased mediation, conflict settlement, and humanitarian support.

3. Transparency and Accountability: Encouraging transparency and accountability in international relations fosters trust and prevents abuses of power. Nations can uphold these principles by adhering to human rights standards, reporting on their actions, and participating in peer reviews.

4. Empowering Developing Nations: Providing technical assistance, capacity-building, and financial support to developing nations empowers them to fully enjoy their equal rights and contribute to the global community.

5. Promoting Education and Cultural Exchange: Enhancing cultural exchange and educational programs fosters mutual understanding and respect among nations, mitigating misunderstandings and prejudices that hinder applying equal rights.

The principle of equal rights among nations is a vital and timeless concept that transcends political boundaries and national interests. It offers a blueprint for fostering global harmony, cooperation, and sustainable development. By embracing the principles of sovereignty, self-determination, non-discrimination, and international cooperation, nations can collectively create a world where peace, justice, and progress prevail. Through diplomacy, strengthening international organizations, promoting transparency, empowering developing nations, and fostering cultural exchange, the promise of equal rights among nations can be realized, paving the way for a more equitable and interconnected future.

HISTORICAL AND CURRENT EXAMPLES OF INEQUALITY AMONG NATIONS

In the vast arena of international relations, where the struggle for dominance and influence unfolds, the principle of equal rights among nations stands as a noble ideal, promising a harmonious world of shared progress. Yet, beneath this aspiration lies a stark reality – the enduring inequalities that cast shadows across the global stage. As historical legacies and contemporary events intersect, an undeniable truth emerges: while the vision of equal rights remains unwavering, the path toward its realization is riddled with complex disparities, historical imprints, and the intricate tapestry of power dynamics.

As the annals of time unfold, historical epochs have etched the genesis of inequality onto the international canvas. The colonial era is an undeniable testament to power dynamics that sowed the seeds of inequality. The scramble for Africa in the late 19th century exemplifies the way colonial powers delineated borders without considering indigenous cultures, leading to enduring conflicts and societal divisions.

The Cold War, an epoch of ideological rivalry between superpowers, further propagated inequality on a global scale. Nations ensnared in the ideological tussle, such as Korea and Vietnam, bore the brunt of proxy conflicts, exacerbating the gulf between East and West. Even as the era of colonization waned, the vestiges of inequality persisted through post-colonial power struggles. Former colonial powers maintained economic leverage, perpetuating neo-colonial practices and resource exploitation, often at the expense of marginalized nations striving for self-determination.

In contemporary realities, echoes of historical inequities reverberate through the present circumstances, underscoring the tenacious nature of this global challenge. Paradoxically, economic disparities persist in a world of abundant resources. Developed nations flaunt prosperity, while impoverished nations grapple with the scourge of poverty. The GDP per capita of affluent nations towers astronomically above their low-income counterparts, perpetuating a glaring economic imbalance.

The COVID-19 pandemic, a defining global event, laid bare the gaping fissures in healthcare equity. Wealthy nations secured swift access to life-saving vaccines, while countless developing nations struggled to secure even basic medical supplies, exposing a dire imbalance in global healthcare access. Amid the information age, technological progress deepens the digital divide. Advanced nations harness technology for societal progress, while marginalized nations confront restricted internet access, amplifying educational and economic inequalities.

The global issue of environmental degradation further underscores inequities. Despite being the primary contributors to climate change, developed nations possess greater resources to adapt, leaving vulnerable nations to bear the brunt of environmental consequences. In a paradox of injustice, inequality often fuels conflicts.

The Syrian civil war is a stark example of socio-economic disparities and political oppression converging, culminating in violent upheaval.

Confronted with the historical roots and contemporary manifestations of inequality, a clarion call to action reverberates. The symphony of history serves as a haunting refrain, reminding humanity that progress is not an inevitable tide. The tapestry of nations remains interwoven with disparities that cast a shadow on the promise of equal rights. Diplomacy, cooperation, and a collective commitment to justice are imperative to transcend this darkness.

Addressing economic disparities demands a shift towards fair trade practices and inclusive economic policies. Strengthening healthcare equity requires a global resolve to ensure equal access to medical resources. Bridging the digital divide mandates concerted efforts to provide universal internet access and technological resources.

Environmental sustainability necessitates international cooperation to mitigate climate change and ensure equitable distribution of its impacts. Confronting historical injustices involves acknowledging the lingering effects of colonialism and working toward redress. As these efforts amalgamate, they can pave the path toward equality among nations.

Charting the Path Forward: Uniting for Equal Rights

In this pursuit of a just and equitable tomorrow, the world finds itself at a crossroads. The complexities embedded within historical inequalities and present-day disparities necessitate bold actions, reimagined strategies, and a relentless commitment to reshaping the global narrative.

The legacy of colonization is a stark reminder that inequality can be deeply entrenched, leaving lasting scars on nations and generations. Acknowledging this painful history is a crucial step toward redressing imbalances. Both economic and symbolic reparations can pave the way for healing wounds that still fester.

Collaborative initiatives are vital to bridge the gaps that history has widened. International aid programs, education exchanges, and technology transfer can empower marginalized nations to stand on an equal footing. By sharing knowledge and resources, the global community can dismantle the barriers that perpetuate inequality.

Economic empowerment also hinges on reforming global trade practices. Restructuring trade agreements to be fair and inclusive can uplift nations historically marginalized in the global economic arena. Such efforts can catalyze sustainable growth, diminish poverty, and contribute to the harmonious coexistence of nations.

The pandemic has brought healthcare access into the spotlight, necessitating transformative changes. International collaborations can enhance healthcare infrastructure, guaranteeing that nations in need are prepared to effectively address health emergencies. The pandemic has emphasized that global health functions as an interconnected system; a vulnerability in one place poses a risk to humanity worldwide.

The digital divide, a pressing concern in the digital age, requires innovative solutions. Initiatives to provide affordable internet access, technological training, and digital resources to underserved communities can narrow the gap and democratize opportunities for education, economic participation, and innovation.

Within the framework of addressing climate change, the concept of common but differentiated responsibilities gains significance. Wealthier countries, given their greater involvement in causing environmental degradation, bear an ethical obligation to support vulnerable nations in adjusting to and mitigating the impacts of climate change. Financing sustainable development and sharing technological advancements can foster a more balanced global response to this shared challenge.

As the threads of history are rewoven with contemporary narratives, international institutions play a pivotal role. The United Nations, among others, serves as a platform for dialogue, cooperation, and conflict resolution. Yet, these institutions must be continually reformed to ensure equitable representation and to prevent powerful nations from exerting undue influence.

A world characterized by equal rights among nations demands a shift in mindset and a collective commitment to justice. Education assumes a pivotal role in steering this transformation. Curricula emphasizing global citizenship, cultural comprehension, and empathy can potentially cultivate generations of individuals committed to eradicating inequalities.

In crafting this just tomorrow, the echoes of history act as both a cautionary tale and a guiding light. The struggles of the past caution us against complacency, while the strides toward justice offer a beacon of hope. It is within humanity's power to disrupt the cycle of inequality and shape a world where nations, regardless of their past or present circumstances, stand as equals.

The journey towards equal rights among nations is a continuous, evolving process. Historical imbalances and present-day inequalities are a call to action rather than a roadblock. Humanity can dismantle the structures that perpetuate inequality by redressing historical injustices, fostering collaboration, and reforming global systems. Through collective efforts driven by the belief in justice and the commitment to shared progress, the symphony of nations can harmonize into a chorus of equality on the global stage.

OVERCOMING HURDLES TO IMPLEMENTING EQUAL RIGHTS GLOBALLY

Pursuing equal rights on a global scale is a noble endeavor that seeks to eradicate the age-old shackles of discrimination, bias, and inequality that have plagued societies for centuries. While the world has made considerable progress in recognizing and advocating for equal rights, numerous hurdles still impede the comprehensive implementation of these rights across all corners of the globe.

Let's delve into these multifaceted challenges that obstruct the relights worldwide while also off innovative strategies to overcome these hurdles and pave the way for a more equitable future.

1. Cultural Diversity and Norms
   One of the most prominent hurdles to implementing equal rights globally is the incredible diversity of cultures, traditions, and norms across different regions and societies. Cultural relativism often poses a challenge, as what may be considered a fundamental right in one culture might be viewed as a breach of norms in another. This divergence can impede the creation of a universally accepted framework for equal rights, as reconciling cultural differences while upholding basic human rights can be complex.

2. Lack of Political Will
   Another significant obstacle lies in governments' and leaders' need for more political will to prioritize and champion equal rights. In many instances, governments prioritize their political agendas over the rights of their citizens, leading to policies and practices that perpetuate inequality. For instance, gender-based discrimination, still rampant in many parts of the world, stems from a lack of political commitment to challenging and changing existing power dynamics.

3. Economic Disparities
   Economic inequalities continue to be a major hurdle toward global equal rights. Socio-economic status often influences access to education, healthcare, and employment opportunities, further deepening existing disparities. Countries with high poverty levels struggle to allocate resources toward social welfare programs that uplift marginalized communities and promote equal rights.

4. Gender Inequality
   Gender discrimination is a persistent barrier to equal rights across the world. Women continue to face unequal pay, limited representation in leadership roles, and systemic violence. Changing deeply ingrained gender norms and biases requires comprehensive

strategies that challenge traditional power structures and promote gender equality early on.

5. Lack of Access to Education
   Education is a fundamental tool for empowerment and the realization of equal rights. However, millions of children worldwide are denied access to quality education due to poverty, conflict, and gender biases. This lack of education perpetuates cycles of inequality, limiting opportunities for individuals to break free from their circumstances.

6. Legal and Judicial Barriers
   While legal frameworks exist to protect equal rights, their implementation and enforcement often fall short. Biased legal systems, corruption, and lack of awareness about rights can hinder progress. Moreover, legal barriers may target specific marginalized groups, including ethnic and religious minorities, refugees, and the LGBTQ+ community, further exacerbating inequality.

Strategies for Overcoming the Hurdles

1. Cultural Sensitivity and Education: Recognizing the diversity of cultures while promoting universal human rights can be achieved through education and awareness campaigns. Governments, NGOs, and international organizations should collaborate to develop culturally sensitive educational materials highlighting the importance of equal rights within various traditions.

2. International Diplomacy and Cooperation: Global issues demand global solutions. International organizations like the United Nations can play a pivotal role in fostering dialogue among nations, encouraging the adoption of universal human rights standards, and promoting cooperation in addressing common challenges.

3. Political Empowerment and Accountability: Citizens must hold their governments responsible for upholding equal rights.

   Civil society groups can be crucial in promoting policies that improve equality and monitoring how well governments are doing in upholding their pledges.

4. Economic Reforms and Social Safety Nets: Governments can implement economic reforms prioritizing poverty alleviation and equitable wealth distribution. By providing social safety nets and investing in education and healthcare, countries can create a more level playing field for all citizens.

5. Promoting Gender Mainstreaming: Integrating gender perspectives into all policies, programs, and projects can help break down barriers to gender equality. Efforts to enhance women's economic, political, and social empowerment can result in a more harmonized and just society.

6. Inclusive Education Initiatives: Governments and organizations should invest in initiatives that ensure quality education for all, particularly focusing on marginalized groups. By promoting inclusivity in education, societies can break the cycle of poverty and discrimination.

7. Strengthening Judicial Systems: Efforts to reform legal systems should be pursued vigorously, including measures to eliminate corruption, enhance transparency, and promote unbiased judgments. Legal literacy programs can empower citizens to understand their rights and navigate the legal system effectively.

The journey toward global equal rights is a complex and multifaceted endeavor, but it is essential for the betterment of humanity. While hurdles may seem insurmountable, a combination of strategic approaches can pave the way for progress. By fostering cross-cultural understanding, advocating for political commitment, addressing economic imbalances, promoting gender equality, ensuring education for all, and reforming legal systems, societies can achieve equal rights for everyone, regardless of their background or circumstances. The key lies in recognizing that this is not a one-size-fits-all endeavor but requires collaborative efforts, innovative solutions, and an unwavering commitment to shaping a more just and equitable world for future generations.

SECURING EQUAL RIGHTS FOR ALL NATIONS: A JOURNEY OF COLLABORATIVE LOVE AND RESPECT

In a world of diversity and complexity, the quest for equal rights among nations is a testament to humanity's yearning for justice and unity. Securing equal rights for all nations is not merely an aspirational goal but a moral imperative that demands visionary leadership, collective efforts, and a foundation rooted in love and respect.

The Essence of Equal Rights for All Nations

At the heart of the concept of equal rights for all nations lies a profound declaration of humanity's interconnectedness and shared destiny. This principle transcends geography, politics' complexities, and economic disparities. It is a rallying cry that resonates with what it means to be human—recognizing that each nation, regardless of its geopolitical stature or economic prowess, holds an inherent worth that cannot be substituted or diminished.

Equal rights for all nations are a beacon of fairness that illuminates the global stage, urging us to cast aside biases and preconceived notions. It embodies the belief that every nation, whether a sprawling powerhouse or a small island community, has an undeniable entitlement to dignity and respect. This principle acknowledges that every individual possesses unique strengths and contributions, and so does every nation offer its distinct narrative, heritage, and potential to enrich the global tapestry.

This concept celebrates self-determination—a sovereign right that empowers nations to carve their destinies free from external coercion. It champions the idea that representation and participation in global affairs should not be confined to a privileged few but extended to all corners of the world. In embracing this ethos, the international community begins building bridges of understanding across languages, ideologies, and borders, fostering unity in diversity.

Ultimately, equal rights for all nations embody the essence of our shared humanity—a reminder that despite our diversity, we are bound by a common thread that transcends the differences that often divide us. It signifies a collective pledge to uphold justice, fairness, and the recognition that our destinies are inexorably intertwined on this intricate canvas.

The Power of Collaborative Love and Respect

The power of collaborative love and respect represents a transformational force that can reshape the landscape of international relations. Beyond mere words, these principles hold the potential to transcend rhetoric and bring about tangible change that resonates across nations. When woven into the fabric of diplomacy, they become more than lofty ideals; they emerge as driving forces capable of catalyzing a new era of global cooperation.

Collaboration, acting as the cornerstone, empowers nations to transcend their capacities and unite for a shared vision of equality. It's a harmonious symphony where diverse nations contribute their unique strengths, knowledge, and resources to orchestrate solutions to complex global challenges. This unity amplifies the impact of their efforts, fostering a sense of shared purpose that defies borders and prevails over divisions.

As a catalyst, love transcends cultural, linguistic, and ideological barriers. It ignites empathy, a profound ability to comprehend the struggles and aspirations of fellow nations. This empathy bridges gaps, cultivating a deep understanding that paves the way for effective collaboration. In the face of disagreement, love encourages world leaders to seek common ground, aligning their actions with the greater good and nurturing an environment where compassion thrives.

Respect, the nurturing soil, fosters an environment where diplomacy flourishes. It's a potent elixir that tempers discourse with civility and upholds the dignity of all parties involved. With respect as the guiding principle, negotiations become a dance of ideas and compromise, devoid of condescension or dominance. This environment of mutual esteem allows for exploring creative solutions and mutual growth.

Unity, collaboration, love, and respect create a synergy that transcends the sum of its parts. They transform international relations into a grand tableau of interconnectedness, where leaders move forward together to secure equal rights for all nations. As this symphony of values resonates across global stages, it carries the potential to not only bring about equitable change but also to redefine the very nature of global discourse. The power of collaborative love and respect is a beacon that beckons us to transform the way we interact to craft a world where the pursuit of equality is rooted in compassion, united effort, and unwavering respect.

Legal Actualization Through Collaboration

1. Reimagining Global Governance Structures
   The first step toward securing equal rights for all nations lies in reimagining and reforming global governance structures. World

leaders can come together to design international organizations that ensure fair representation and decision-making for all nations, irrespective of their economic or political stature. Collaborative initiatives can lead to the equitable distribution of leadership roles and voting mechanisms that empower smaller nations to shape global policies actively.

2. Enforcing Universal Legal Standards
   Collaboration among world leaders can manifest in enforcing universal legal standards that promote equal rights among nations. Nations can pledge to uphold principles of non-discrimination, sovereignty, and mutual respect through international treaties and agreements. Creating an international court dedicated to addressing disputes related to equal rights violations can provide a platform for impartial judgment and resolution.

3. Empowering Diplomatic Peacemaking
   Diplomacy steeped in love and respect can be a potent tool for securing equal rights for all nations. World leaders, driven by a shared commitment to fairness, can engage in diplomatic peacemaking efforts to resolve conflicts and prevent further escalation. Mediation and dialogue can help dismantle barriers and misunderstandings, fostering cooperation rather than confrontation.

4. Promoting Equitable Trade and Economic Relations
   Equal rights among nations extend to economic realms as well. Collaborative efforts by world leaders can lead to formulation of trade agreements that promote fairness and economic growth for all nations. Leaders can foster an environment of shared prosperity by reducing trade barriers and supporting capacity-building in economically disadvantaged nations.

5. Education and Cultural Exchange
   Collaborative initiatives in education and cultural exchange can nurture a sense of interconnectedness and solidarity among nations. Educational programs that promote global citizenship education can instill in individuals the values of empathy, tolerance, and equal respect for all nations. Cultural exchanges can dismantle stereotypes and bridge cultural gaps, fostering genuine understanding.

6. Addressing Environmental and Humanitarian Crises
   The global challenges of environmental degradation and humanitarian crises require united efforts to secure equal rights for all nations. Collective endeavors, such as global agreements for mitigating climate change and providing assistance during disasters, can demonstrate world leaders' dedication to protecting the welfare and rights of all countries, particularly those facing a disproportionate impact.

Securing equal rights for all nations is not a fleeting aspiration; it is a journey that requires the unwavering dedication of world leaders. Collaborative efforts guided by love and respect can transform this aspiration into a reality. As world leaders stand united, bound by the shared values of justice and fairness, they can reshape the global landscape. By reimagining governance structures, enforcing legal standards, embracing diplomacy, promoting equitable economic relations, fostering education and cultural exchange, and addressing global challenges, world leaders can weave a tapestry of equality that is a testament to humanity's collective potential.

The journey to securing equal rights for all nations is not solely a legal or political endeavor but a reflection of our shared humanity. It is a declaration that every nation's voice matters, that no nation should be left behind, and that collaboration founded on love and respect is the key to building a world where justice, unity, and equality prevail. Through these collaborative efforts, world leaders can create a legacy that resonates across generations, inspiring a world where equal rights are not just a concept but a living reality nurtured by the bonds of love and respect that unite us all.

CHAPTER FIVE

SOVEREIGNTY AND COOPERATION

The interplay between sovereignty and cooperation weaves a story of complexity, unity, and the quest for a harmonious global order. Sovereignty, the cherished principle that grants nations autonomy over their internal affairs, stands as a beacon of identity and self-determination. Simultaneously, cooperation serves as a bridge that connects disparate nations, fostering shared progress and mutual understanding. The juxtaposition of these two concepts encapsulates the delicate dance between individuality and interconnectedness on the world stage.

Like a nation's cultural DNA, sovereignty is a cornerstone of modern nation-states. It signifies the right to shape domestic policies, chart independent trajectories, and safeguard unique identities. Nations have fiercely defended their sovereignty throughout history, reflecting a primal urge to govern their destinies free from external coercion. This assertion of autonomy often intertwines with pursuing equal rights and dismantling colonial legacies, spotlighting the struggle for a just global landscape.

Cooperation, however, emerges as a counterpoint to the solitary stance of sovereignty. It recognizes that the challenges of the modern era are often too colossal for any nation to confront in isolation. Climate change, pandemics, terrorism—these are but a few examples that transcend borders, demanding collective efforts. Cooperation mandates a willingness to transcend differences, join hands across oceans and ideologies, and find common ground in pursuing shared solutions. It's a testament to humanity's interconnectedness, emphasizing that the fate of one nation invariably ripples through the destinies of others.

The intricate balance between sovereignty and cooperation unveils a multifaceted narrative that necessitates nations to be both architects of their destinies and custodians of the global commons. As our world becomes increasingly intertwined through technological advancements and cultural exchanges, the understanding that sovereignty need not come at the cost of cooperation becomes pivotal. The art lies in navigating this duality, in wielding sovereignty responsibly while embracing the potential of collaborative endeavors.

In this chapter, we will explore how nations grapple with the tension between self-governance and global unity, how they reconcile their narratives with the broader symphony of international relations, and how the harmony between sovereignty and cooperation may just hold the key to a more prosperous and peaceful world. This exploration transcends theoretical discourse; it delves into the heart of diplomatic negotiations, socio-economic partnerships, and the essence of human endeavor in pursuing a better tomorrow.

THE INTERPLAY BETWEEN SOVEREIGNTY AND EFFECTIVE GLOBAL COOPERATION

The concepts of sovereignty and effective global cooperation are threads woven together, creating a complex and captivating pattern that defines the very essence of our interconnected existence. As two dancers engaged in a graceful but intricate duet, these notions twirl and intertwine, crafting a narrative that spans politics, identity, and progress.

Sovereignty, with its roots deeply embedded in the history of nations, stands as a symbol of selfhood and independence. The sovereign power paints the distinct hues on a country's canvas, allowing it to paint its destiny, design its laws, and shape its culture. Yet, as the world continues to shrink due to technological advancements and the flow of ideas, sovereignty shares the stage with an equally compelling partner—effective global cooperation.

In the theater of contemporary challenges, from climate change's unrelenting crescendo to the crescendo of economic interdependence, the isolation of nations is but an illusion. The whisper of one nation's choices reverberates across borders, creating a symphony of consequences that knows no geographic bounds. In such a symphony, effective global cooperation takes center stage, adorned with the urgency of shared solutions and the melody of collective prosperity. The global challenges of our time transcend the neat borders drawn on maps, and in response, the hands of nations must stretch across those lines to join in a collaborative dance of survival and advancement.

The Essence of Identity and Autonomy

At the heart of each nation's existence lies the principle of sovereignty, an intricate tapestry woven through the annals of history. Much like the foundation of a magnificent building, sovereignty serves as the bedrock upon which a nation's unique identity is erected, allowing it to stand tall and resolute on the global stage. This foundational principle enshrined both in the pages of international law and in the collective psyche of nations, bestows upon each entity the sacrosanct right to chart its course without external coercion. Within these borders, cultures flourish, languages thrive, and destinies take shape, forming the vibrant mosaic of humanity's diverse tapestry.

While sovereignty affords nations their distinctiveness and autonomy, it does not exist in isolation nor render states impervious to the currents of an interconnected world. The threads of our existence have been intricately woven together by the hands of time and technological advancement. The choices made within one nation's borders ripple outward, crossing frontiers and affecting distant shores. The rise and fall of economies, the shared burden of global challenges like climate change and pandemics, and the swift currents of cross-border migration all attest to the inescapable reality of our interdependence.

The necessity of effective global cooperation resonates as a compelling refrain in this symphony of nations. The melodies of shared solutions and joint endeavors harmonize with the principles of sovereignty, acknowledging that geographical boundaries do not confine the world's challenges. From the negotiation tables of climate agreements to the collaborative efforts in vaccine distribution, the recognition that the fate of one nation is irrevocably tied to the fate of others becomes evident. Effective global cooperation, like the skilled conductor of an orchestra, orchestrates the harmonious blending of autonomy and interconnectedness, allowing the diverse voices of nations to create a symphony that transcends the limitations of individual notes.

In this narrative, the interplay between sovereignty and effective global cooperation remains both a challenge and an opportunity. It beckons nations to find equilibrium between safeguarding their identities and embracing the call for collective action. It implores leaders to recognize that the pursuit of autonomy need not come at the cost of collaboration and that in unity; the strength of individual nations can be magnified to conquer challenges that know no borders. Thus, the essence of identity and autonomy, entwined with the imperative of global cooperation, continues to shape the story of our shared human journey.

Effective Global Cooperation

The emergence of challenges that transcend geographical boundaries serves as a resounding wake-up call, compelling nations to bridge the gaps of sovereignty with the bonds of effective global cooperation. In an era where the tapestry of humanity is intricately woven, the urgency to collaborate resonates with unprecedented clarity. From the ominous specter of climate change, which knows no borders and threatens the very ecosystem that sustains us, to the swift and unrelenting spread of infectious diseases, which pay no heed to political demarcations, the imperatives of unity and shared effort become glaringly evident.

Effective global cooperation entails a symphony of nations harmonizing their disparate notes into a melody of shared solutions. It's a grand orchestra where diverse nations contribute their unique instruments—wisdom, resources, and effort—to create a composition that resonate with the symphonic power of collective action. This cooperation, exemplified through esteemed institutions like the United Nations and the World Health Organization and pivotal international agreements like the Paris Agreement, is a testament to humanity's ability to transcend self-interest and embrace the common good.

In this arena of global collaboration, negotiation, and compromise take center stage. The interplay of differing perspectives and priorities weaves a rich tapestry of diplomatic discourse, ultimately creating frameworks that address multifaceted challenges. As one nation's prosperity and security are inextricably linked to the well-being of its counterparts, the concept of shared destiny becomes a driving force. Just as the human body thrives when its various parts work in harmonious synergy, so does the global community flourish when nations unite in purposeful cooperation.

In the annals of history, this era will be remembered not only for the complexities of its challenges but also for the triumphs of collective action. The pages of tomorrow's books will recount stories of collaboration that transcended borders, illustrating how nations set aside differences and forged pathways to secure a brighter future in the spirit of solidarity. This narrative of effective global cooperation stands as a testament to humanity's capacity to rise above divisions and harness the power of unity in pursuing a shared destiny.

Synergies and Benefits

The harmonious relationship between sovereignty and effective global cooperation sets the stage for a remarkable synergy, a dynamic interplay that propels nations towards collective triumphs while safeguarding their identities. This alliance isn't a zero-sum game; rather, it's a strategic convergence where collaboration amplifies strengths and unlocks potential that transcends the boundaries of individual capabilities.

Cooperation bears fruit not only through shared accomplishments but also through the blossoming of mutual benefits. By aligning their efforts, nations can achieve outcomes far beyond the confines of their sovereignty's reach. Innovation unfurls its wings when the wellspring of knowledge, best practices, and cutting-edge technologies converge. This innovation, nurtured by the collective wisdom of diverse perspectives, becomes the cornerstone of progress that benefits all, regardless of size, status, or geographic location.

Moreover, the symphony of cooperative initiatives resounds with diplomatic overtones. The bridges built through such endeavors echo the rhythms of camaraderie and understanding. Nations that might otherwise have remained isolated find common ground on shared goals, exchanging resources and ideas, fostering cross-cultural enrichment, and nurturing cross-border relationships. This interconnectedness molds a world where geopolitical frictions can be mollified through the exchange of mutual respect and collaboration.

The European Union (EU) stands as an exemplary testament to the efficacy of this harmonious relationship. In this union of sovereign states, national identities remain steadfast while the benefits of collaborative synergy are reaped. The EU isn't a dilution of sovereignty but rather an embodiment of its strategic embodiment. Nations have pooled their strengths here to forge a formidable economic and political entity. This alliance showcases how sovereignty and cooperation, far from adversarial, can amplify one another's impact.

Within the EU, diverse nations resonate in harmony, amplifying their voices through collective endeavors in trade, security, and shared values. This cooperative ecosystem not only exemplifies the success of the synergy between sovereignty and collaboration but also illuminates the path forward for nations seeking to navigate the complex tapestry of an interconnected world.

In the grand theater of international relations, the synergy between sovereignty and effective global cooperation is a symphony in which each nation, an individual instrument, plays its part in enriching the collective composition. Through this harmonious interplay, the world moves closer to realizing the potential embedded within the realm of unity. This orchestration yields rewards that no individual sovereign state could achieve alone.

Challenges and Complexities

A realm of limitless potential exists within effective global cooperation, but it is not without its labyrinthine challenges and intricate complexities. While the allure of shared achievements beckons nations to unite, navigating the multifaceted terrain of collaboration requires a deft hand and an unwavering commitment to finding harmonious resolutions amidst divergent interests.

One of the most formidable challenges arises from the divergence in interpreting shared objectives. As nations join hands to tackle complex global issues, differing perspectives can lead to conflicts in defining the very goals they seek to achieve. Discord might emerge when nuances of priorities and aspirations are laid bare, requiring a delicate orchestration of dialogue and compromise to ensure that the collective pursuit remains focused and aligned.

The distribution of benefits is another thorny thicket to navigate. In the mosaic of collaboration, questions of who bears what burdens and reaps what rewards are inevitable. Diverse economies, resource availability, and varying levels of development can engender disparities in the benefits accrued from cooperative efforts. Negotiating this distribution fairly demands understanding each nation's unique circumstances and a commitment to rectifying inequalities for sustainable and inclusive progress.

Yet, perhaps the most intricate dance occurs around the issue of sovereignty. Nations hold their autonomy dearly, and the concept of ceding even a modicum can be met with apprehension. Striking a balance between preserving national identity and participating in cooperative endeavors requires the adept navigation of political, cultural, and economic sensitivities. Pursuing shared solutions demands a harmonious blend of principled stands and pragmatic adjustments—a symphony of diplomacy that resonates with mutual respect and understanding.

Nowhere is this intricate interplay more evident than in matters of security. The tension between safeguarding national interests and engaging in collective security arrangements exposes the heart of the complexity. While nations recognize the imperative of shared security in an interconnected world, concerns about compromising sovereignty and becoming entangled in foreign entanglements often arise. Striking the right balance here is an ardent quest for both self-preservation and the greater good—a quest that underscores the gravity of choices nations must make.

In global cooperation, the challenges and complexities serve as the chiaroscuro, casting shadows and illumination. They demand a steady hand, strategic foresight, and a willingness to traverse the intricate nuances of international relations. However, nations forge their mettle through these challenges, proving their commitment to the collective and uncovering the rich tapestry of collaborative potential beneath the surface. As the world evolves, so must the approach to these challenges, recognizing that the delicate interplay between sovereignty and cooperation is a canvas for creativity, compromise, and the continual pursuit of a more united and harmonious world.

Nurturing a Balanced Future

As our world advances through the currents of time, the delicate choreography between sovereignty and effective global cooperation remains at the forefront of shaping the destiny of nations. In this ongoing dance, striking a harmonious equilibrium demands far-sighted leadership, robust dialogue, and the agility to pivot in response to the ever-evolving landscape of challenges and opportunities. It's a process that hinges on recognizing that while sovereignty constitutes the bedrock of national identity, cooperation is the vessel through which progress can be navigated.

In this complex balance, multilateralism emerges as a beacon of guidance. Multilateral institutions and agreements provide the framework within which nations can collectively address the complexities that transcend borders while safeguarding their respective sovereignty. The United Nations Sustainable Development Goals stand as a testament to the potential of multilateralism.

Countries unite to confront universal challenges such as poverty, inequality, and environmental degradation, recognizing that a collective approach can yield transformative outcomes.

Likewise, the global response to the escalating threat of cybercrime underscores the efficacy of multilateral approaches. As digital realms transcend physical borders, the multilateral collaboration of nations becomes a strategic necessity and a means of preserving individual sovereignty in an increasingly interconnected landscape. Through shared frameworks and cooperative endeavors, nations can bolster their defenses while enhancing the security and autonomy of their digital domains.

Within the orchestration of sovereignty and cooperation, the harmonious interplay of compromise, dialogue, and adaptability gives rise to a resonating melody that reverberates within the chambers of diplomacy and global relations. Cultivating equilibrium for the future requires more than simply acknowledging the intricate tensions in motion; it mandates a steadfast dedication to the greater good, a readiness to transcend narrow viewpoints, and a profound realization that the path to advancement is most effectively navigated through collaborative efforts.

As the world scripts its narrative, the interplay between sovereignty and effective global cooperation remains an ever-evolving script, with each nation contributing its unique verse to the grand chorus of humanity's collective journey. Through the lens of multilateralism, this symphony gains depth and resonance, illuminating the path to a more equitable, secure, and interconnected future. In this future, nations, while maintaining their sovereignty, rise to the challenge of collaboration and make harmonious strides toward shared goals.

The interplay between sovereignty and effective global cooperation is a complex dance that encapsulates the essence of international relations. Nations, like individual instruments in an orchestra, each bring their unique melodies to the global stage. The harmonious symphony emerges when these melodies intersect, creating a cacophony of shared goals, collaborative efforts, and progress that resonates far beyond national borders.

The challenges are formidable, but so are the opportunities. By embracing the synergy between sovereignty and effective global cooperation, nations can navigate the turbulent waters of our interconnected world with wisdom, foresight, and a commitment to collective prosperity. In this symphony of nations, the interplay between sovereignty and cooperation becomes a testament to the power of collaboration – a force that transcends boundaries enriches identities and propels humanity toward a more harmonious future.

NAVIGATING CHALLENGES IN BALANCING NATIONAL AUTONOMY AND GLOBAL UNITY

Navigating the delicate balance between national autonomy and the call for unified action on the global stage is a journey rife with complexities, an artful tightrope walk that requires the finesse of a diplomat, the foresight of a strategist, and the heart of a visionary.

Imagine the world as a grand tapestry woven with threads of diverse nations, each representing a unique identity, culture, and aspiration. These threads converge and diverge, intertwining in a magnificent display of human complexity. Sovereignty, the vibrant hue defining each thread, is a sentinel for a nation's autonomy. This sovereign power allows it to shape its destiny, weave its laws, and draw the boundaries of its narrative. This sovereignty renders each nation an independent brushstroke on the global canvas, unique yet part of a larger masterpiece.

However, the world's canvas has evolved into a vast, interconnected mural where challenges like climate change, pandemics, and cyber threats ignore borders as they traverse the terrain. In this age of instant connectivity, the juxtaposition between safeguarding autonomy and the clarion call for united efforts is undeniable. While sovereignty is the heartbeat of a nation, effective global cooperation is the symphony of heartbeats converging into a rhythm that resonates across borders, pushing nations to collaborate for solutions that transcend their scope.

One must envision a diplomatic ballet to grasp the intricacies of this interplay. The stage is set with nations representing characters, each waltzing with its identity, culture, and goals. Disagreements arise, resembling intricate footwork, as nations interpret shared objectives through their unique lens. Dialogues are the graceful spins that navigate this choreography, seeking common ground amidst the elaborate choreography of interests.

As this dance progresses, a collaborative duet emerge, where the nuanced steps of compromise and adaptability intertwine with the leaps of innovative solutions. This synergy isn't a dilution of sovereignty but a harmonious crescendo where the collective becomes more potent than the individual. The European Union is a monument to this harmony, a consortium of nations that retain their identity while leveraging collective strength for economic, political, and security endeavors.

Yet, this harmony has its dissonances. The complexities unfurl in the security spotlight, where nations grapple with the tension between safeguarding autonomy and participating in global defense alliances. The scales of equilibrium teeter a delicate act that demands wisdom in discerning when to unite for collective security while respecting the essence of sovereignty.

The paradox deepens when navigating shared objectives. In this intricate waltz, nations must harmonize their interpretations of overarching goals while finding balance in distributing the benefits of collaboration. The ripples of this collaboration extend beyond economics, forging diplomatic bridges between nations that might have otherwise remained distant.

This interplay, a captivating sonnet of tensions and unity, is adorned with multilateralism garlands. Multilateral institutions and agreements offer a stage for nations to showcase their individuality while pursuing common objectives. The United Nations Sustainable Development Goals exemplify this by stitching aspirations for global progress into a tapestry that respects the sovereignty of each participating nation.

As the curtains draw on this captivating performance, the script of balancing national autonomy and global unity remains open-ended. It is a saga of challenges and triumphs, complexities and simplicities, woven together like the myriad threads of a tapestry. It is a testament to human capacity – the ability to reconcile the seemingly irreconcilable, to harmonize the individual notes into a symphony of shared progress.

The interplay between sovereignty and global cooperation is the orchestration of a world in transformation. It's the evolution of diplomacy in an era of connectivity, a narrative that tells the tale of nations navigating through the labyrinthine corridors of autonomy and unity. It's a narrative that reinforces the realization that while national identities remain distinct, pursuing common objectives can amplify their impact.

Navigating these challenges isn't just a political or diplomatic endeavor; it's a testament to the depths of human potential. It reflects our ability to transcend borders, forge connections, and seek solutions beyond the confines of our immediate surroundings. It's a testament to the symphony of collaboration that weaves our diverse identities into the fabric of a shared future.

COLLABORATIVE DIPLOMACY

A fascinating interplay between sovereignty and cooperation has emerged, leading to compelling instances of effective collaborative diplomacy. The delicate equilibrium between upholding national autonomy and engaging in cooperative endeavors to tackle global challenges has resulted in remarkable outcomes across diverse domains.

The Arctic Council, established in 1996, stands as a prime model of nations collectively addressing shared concerns while respecting individual sovereignty. The council has adeptly navigated environmental concerns and sustainable development by comprising eight Arctic states and indigenous organizations. Research from the Arctic Monitoring and Assessment Programme (AMAP) highlights the efficacy of collaborative initiatives within the council. For instance, the Arctic Climate Impact Assessment, driven by scientific cooperation, has provided critical insights into climate change's impact on the region. This scientific collaboration underscores the belief that collective knowledge and coordinated action are crucial in safeguarding national interests, exemplifying the potential of the sovereignty-cooperation nexus.

The European Union (EU), a monumental experiment in integration, epitomizes the transformative potential of the sovereignty-cooperation nexus. Historical analysis by economists Jeffrey Sachs and Andrew Warner underscores how the EU's commitment to cooperation has contributed to economic growth and political stability. Creating a single market, a common currency, and harmonized regulations within the EU have fostered an environment where nations willingly cede aspects of sovereignty for the greater good. Empirical research by Alberto Alesina and Enrico Spolaore highlights how supranational institutions facilitate cooperation by addressing externalities that could impede cross-border collaboration. The EU's success offers a profound lesson: judicious relinquishment of sovereignty can yield immense benefits through shared endeavors.

Global health challenges serve as a compelling testament to the necessity of international cooperation. Analysis of the World Health

Organization's (WHO) role during pandemics reveals how shared information and resources enable nations to respond effectively. Empirical studies on HIV/AIDS cooperation, such as research by Sophie Harman, emphasize that pooling resources and expertise across countries has been pivotal in curbing the epidemic. The WHO's International Health Regulations demonstrate how nations can harmonize their approaches to global health security. The data-driven success of these initiatives underscores the power of collaborative diplomacy in safeguarding public health.

The realm of space exploration showcases a distinctive frontier for the sovereignty-cooperation nexus. Analysis of the International Space Station (ISS) underscores how countries like the United States, Russia, and European nations engage in joint research and technology sharing to operate the station. Research by Joan Johnson-Freese demonstrates that this collaborative approach lowers costs and facilitates knowledge exchange. The Outer Space Treaty, ratified by 110 countries, exemplifies the commitment to peaceful space exploration while respecting national sovereignty. This cooperative space venture exemplifies how nations can achieve scientific progress and technological advancement by transcending territorial boundaries.

Environmental challenges necessitate transnational solutions rooted in the sovereignty-cooperation nexus. Analysis of the Paris Agreement reveals how countries align their national climate goals within a global framework. Thiemo Fetzer's research underscores that collaborative climate action mitigates the "free-riding" predicament in which certain nations might capitalize on the efforts of others. Empirical evidence from the International Renewable Energy Agency (IRENA) studies demonstrates that integrating renewable energy technologies exemplifies how joint investments foster sustainable development.

The sovereignty-cooperation nexus is a compelling paradigm for international relations in a rapidly changing world. A rigorous analysis of successful instances underscores a consistent pattern: strategic collaboration yields tangible benefits that transcend the limitations of individual nation-states. Historical data, empirical research, and evidence-based insights collectively reinforce the notion that while sovereignty remains integral, cooperation enhances global outcomes.

This nuanced balance demands meticulous negotiation and adherence to shared values. Trust, transparent communication, and the pragmatic recognition of mutual interdependence underpin the effectiveness of collaborative diplomacy. As the dynamics of the world stage keep changing, the insights drawn from these occurrences point the way toward a more interconnected future founded on collaboration.

The nexus between sovereignty and collaboration represents a period of collective advancement in the vast tapestry of international relations. The concepts illustrated by these examples provide a road map for maximizing the power of unity as nations traverse difficult circumstances. The examples of successful collaboration remind us that, despite the complexity and unpredictability of global dynamics, we can work together to create a more enlightened, affluent, and peaceful world.

FORGING A NEW PARADIGM

A revolutionary paradigm that transcends the traditional bounds of sovereignty and ushers in an age of collaborative growth is developing in the complex web of international interactions. The idea of using sovereignty to spur global progress is gaining popularity as countries struggle with global problems that go beyond national boundaries. This paradigm shift signifies a break from the conventional view of sovereignty as an impenetrable barrier and embraces it as a driver for collaboration and improvement on a global scale.

This new paradigm's heart lies in the reconciliation of sovereignty and collaboration. Historically, sovereignty has been considered the cornerstone of nation-states, the defining factor that sets them apart in a complex world. Yet, in an era marked by climate change, pandemics, and technological interconnectivity, the sanctity of borders is challenged. The Covid-19 pandemic, for instance, laid bare the stark reality that global challenges demand global solutions. The swift and efficient dissemination of information, medical supplies, and vaccines required nations to set aside rigid notions of sovereignty in favor of collaborative action. This underscores the notion that while sovereignty remains intrinsic, it can be harnessed as a catalyst for meaningful collaboration.

The traditional sovereignty paradigm often perpetuated a zero-sum game, where nations viewed each other as rivals competing for finite resources and power. However, a shift is underway as humanity's challenges become more complex. Sovereignty has transitioned from being a hindrance to becoming a cornerstone upon which collaborative endeavors can be constructed.

For instance, the Paris Climate Agreement illustrates how countries use their sovereignty to set shared objectives and pool resources for environmental sustainability.

The alliance formed by the European Union, once a conglomerate of rival nations, showcases how shared interests can transcend historical animosities, creating a harmonious collaboration ecosystem. This shift signals that sovereignty, rather than a barrier, can be the catalyst that fuels collaborative progress.

The new paradigm necessitates departing fragmented decision-making towards integrated approaches that acknowledge shared responsibilities. Realizing that challenges like cybersecurity, terrorism, and global health require collective solutions has prompted a reevaluation of sovereignty's role. Establishing international organizations such as the United Nations, the World Health Organization, and INTERPOL reflects the acknowledgment that sovereignty is not an impediment but a conduit forging a safer and more stable world. Research from the Global Governance Project underscores that these organizations have become vehicles for nations to pool their sovereignty, creating global norms, standards, and responses. This integration signifies that leveraging sovereignty can amplify collaborative potential.

In an age characterized by digital interconnectedness, sovereignty takes on new dimensions. Cyberspace, the global digital realm, knows no geographical boundaries and transcends traditional definitions of territoriality. Nations grapple with the need to protect their digital landscapes while collaborating to combat cyber threats that emanate beyond their borders. Cyber policy experts' research illustrates how nations harness sovereignty as a tool to create cyber norms, regulations, and collaborative frameworks. This dynamic illustrates that sovereignty is no longer confined to physical borders but extends into the virtual realm, where cooperation is equally crucial.

The advent of this new paradigm brings with it a multitude of opportunities. The dynamic shift from unilateral to collaborative action amplifies the impact of policies, technologies, and innovations. The emergence of the Fourth Industrial Revolution, characterized by advancements in artificial intelligence, biotechnology, and renewable energy, provides a vivid example of how nations can collectively utilize their sovereignty to confront critical global issues. Extensively researched studies conducted by the World Economic Forum highlight that these technological breakthroughs carry the capacity to narrow disparities, propel inclusive development, and mold a future in which sovereignty becomes a catalyst for mutual advancement.

Leveraging sovereignty for collaborative progress is challenging. Striking a balance between national interests and global welfare demands adept negotiation and pragmatic decision-making. Skeptics argue that relinquishing too much sovereignty could lead to the erosion of national identity and autonomy. However, the success of initiatives like the Sustainable Development Goals (SDGs) reveals that collaboration need not come at the expense of sovereignty. By aligning national policies with overarching global objectives, nations can simultaneously uphold their sovereignty while contributing to a more equitable world.

In the annals of human history, epochs are marked by paradigm shifts that alter the course of civilization. The current shift, where sovereignty becomes a conduit for collaborative progress, stands as a transformative juncture. Thorough research, creative writing, and critical thinking converge to illuminate a landscape where sovereignty is no longer a barrier but a bridge connecting nations in pursuit of shared goals. As the challenges of the 21st century continue to test humanity's resolve, leveraging sovereignty for collaborative progress emerges as a beacon of hope, guiding nations toward a future defined by unity, cooperation, and collective destiny.

CHAPTER SIX

MULTILATERAL AGREEMENTS AND EQUALITY OF VOTES

In the labyrinth of international diplomacy, where diverse nations converge to tackle global challenges, Multilateral Agreements and Equality of Votes emerge as a cornerstone of equitable collaboration. As the world navigates intricate webs of interdependence and mutual interests, the significance of multilateral agreements cannot be overstated. These agreements, akin to symphonies composed of diverse voices, harmonize the aspirations and efforts of nations toward shared goals.

Central to this discourse is the principle of "Equality of Votes," an embodiment of democracy on the global stage. In a realm where the powers of nations vary vastly, the concept underscores the belief that every voice, regardless of size or influence, holds intrinsic value. The scale may differ, but the vote remains an equalizer, a beacon guiding negotiations and fostering inclusivity.

This chapter explores the dynamic interplay between multilateral agreements and the fundamental tenet of equal voting rights. It delves into the historical tapestry where nations converged to address issues that transcend borders, showcasing the metamorphosis of diplomacy from a bilateral affair to a collaborative symposium of nations. The chapter navigates through the annals of time, illuminating milestones where multilateral agreements paved the way for innovative solutions, laying the groundwork for a fairer, more balanced world order.

The threads of this discussion weave through the intricacies of diplomacy, shedding light on how international conventions and treaties have forged alliances that transcend individual interests. It dissects the nuances of negotiations where countries, each armed with an equal vote, engage in the intricate dance of compromise and consensus-building. From climate accords to trade agreements, the power of multilateralism and equal votes resounds, shaping the global landscape one resolution at a time.

THE EVOLUTION AND EFFICACY OF MULTILATERAL AGREEMENTS

The concept of multilateral agreements, also known as international treaties or conventions involving multiple nations, has evolved significantly throughout history. These agreements are pivotal in fostering cooperation, resolving disputes, and promoting shared goals among nations. The efficacy of multilateral agreements has been a subject of intense scholarly discourse.

The historical evolution of multilateral agreements is a tapestry woven with the threads of human interaction, diplomacy, and the changing dynamics of global politics. This journey through time reveals how these agreements have transformed from informal alliances of antiquity to the cornerstone of modern international relations.

In the annals of history, the roots of multilateral agreements can be traced to the early civilizations that sought to establish cooperative frameworks for mutual benefit. Empires, city-states, and tribal societies engaged in treaties and alliances for myriad purposes, ranging from military collaborations and trade facilitation to diplomatic dialogue. While often informal and context-specific, these agreements laid the groundwork for the principles of cooperation and mutual understanding that underpin contemporary multilateral diplomacy.

Nevertheless, the rise of modern international law brought multilateral agreements into a formalized and organized realm. A crucial juncture in this development was the Peace of Westphalia in 1648, a collection of treaties that signaled the conclusion of the Thirty Years' War and the Eighty Years' War. These treaties introduced the concept of state sovereignty, recognizing individual states' autonomy and territorial integrity. Moreover, they laid the foundation for the non-interference principle in other state's internal affairs, a cornerstone of multilateral agreements that persists today.

The 20th century heralded a seismic shift in the landscape of multilateral agreements, largely in response to the cataclysmic events of World War I and World War II. The League of Nations, established after the Great War, represented a collective endeavor to prevent future conflicts through diplomacy, cooperation, and collective security. While the League aimed to promote global harmony, its efficacy could have been improved by various factors, including the absence of key powers like the United States and the limited ability to enforce its decisions.

The aftermath of World War II brought forth an even more robust and comprehensive international institution – the United Nations (UN). Founded in 1945, the UN emerged as a multifaceted forum for addressing the international community's challenges. With an expanded mandate encompassing peace, security, development, and human rights, the UN marked a watershed moment in the evolution of multilateral agreements. It represented an audacious effort to harness the collective power of nations to prevent further global conflict, promote socio-economic progress, and safeguard human dignity.

The historical journey of multilateral agreements is characterized by an evolution from informal alliances to formal treaties, from diplomatic negotiations to structured international organizations. This serves as proof of the ever-evolving terrain of global politics, humanity's desire for harmony and teamwork, and the continuous endeavor to strike a balance between national independence and international collaboration. As our world navigates complex challenges, the historical evolution of multilateral agreements stands as evidence of the potential inherent in collaborative diplomacy and the impact of shared ambitions on shaping history.

Role of Multilateral Agreements in Promoting Equality Among Nations

Multilateral agreements serve as dynamic instruments in international relations, fostering equality among nations. As the global stage continues to evolve, these agreements stand as powerful mechanisms that transcend borders, cultures, and political ideologies. Their pivotal role in promoting equality among nations is underscored by the principles they embody and the avenues they provide for nations to collaborate.

The following are how multilateral agreements contribute to the achievement of equality on the international stage:

- Normative Framework for Equality
  Multilateral agreements establish a normative structure that sets forth regulations, standards, and principles universally applicable to all nations involved.

  This system guarantees that no country is free from the commitments outlined in the agreement. The UN General Assembly, for instance, emphasized the inherent equality of all people and the significance of non-discrimination, regardless of country, in the Universal Declaration of Human Rights, which was approved in 1948.

- Equal Participation and Representation
  Multilateral agreements often require the equal participation of all member nations in decision-making processes. This democratic principle ensures that the interests of smaller and less powerful nations are not overshadowed by those of larger and more influential states. The United Nations General Assembly exemplifies this by affording each member state an equal vote, regardless of size or economic strength.

- Addressing Global Challenges
  Multilateral agreements serve as platforms for nations to collectively address global challenges that transcend borders, such as climate change, infectious diseases, terrorism, and nuclear proliferation. These agreements acknowledge that these issues affect all nations, regardless of their economic, political, or military power, emphasizing common but differentiated responsibilities.

- Conflict Resolution and Peacekeeping
  Multilateral agreements play a vital role in conflict resolution and peacekeeping efforts. Through mechanisms like the International Court of Justice and peacekeeping missions authorized by the UN Security Council, nations can seek impartial arbitration and intervention in disputes, ensuring that weaker nations are not subjected to the unilateral decisions of stronger ones.

Efficacy of Multilateral Agreements in Promoting Equality

While the concept of multilateral agreements holds great promise for promoting equality among nations, their efficacy is subject to various challenges and criticisms:

1. Power Imbalances
   One of the major challenges lies in the persistence of power imbalances among nations. Stronger and more influential nations

often wield disproportionate influence in negotiations and decision-making processes. This can lead to unequal implementation and enforcement of agreements, undermining equality.

2. Non-Compliance and Selective Implementation
   Some nations may selectively implement or disregard the terms of multilateral agreements, especially if they perceive their national interests as being compromised. This non-compliance undermines the effectiveness of agreements and hampers the achievement of equality.

3. Lack of Enforcement Mechanisms
   Many multilateral agreements need robust enforcement mechanisms. While some agreements empower international bodies like the UN Security Council to impose sanctions or use force in case of violations, these mechanisms often need to be improved by geopolitical considerations and great power politics.

4. Cultural and Contextual Differences
   Multilateral agreements must consider participating nations' diverse cultural, political, and economic contexts. What may be considered equitable and fair in one cultural context might not necessarily hold for another. This challenge requires careful consideration to avoid imposing norms that do not respect the equality of diverse nations.

The evolution of multilateral agreements represents a remarkable development in international relations, fostering cooperation and shared goals among nations. Their role in promoting equality among nations is evident through establishing normative frameworks, equal participation, and pursuing common objectives. However, challenges such as power imbalances, non-compliance, and the need for enforcement mechanisms raise questions about their efficacy in achieving true equality.

Efforts to enhance the efficacy of multilateral agreements should focus on addressing power imbalances, strengthening enforcement mechanisms, and ensuring inclusivity in decision-making processes. Fostering a culture of respect for diverse perspectives and contexts is crucial for achieving equality among nations through multilateral agreements. While they may not be a panacea, multilateral agreements remain indispensable for creating a more just and equitable global order.

EVALUATING THE ROLE OF VOTING EQUALITY IN GLOBAL DECISION-MAKING

The quest for global equality is complex, with variations in cultures, economies, and political systems. The idea of vote equality in international decision-making processes is the foundation of this attempt. The necessity of equitable representation for all countries becomes center stage as the need for international collaboration and diplomacy in resolving transboundary concerns like climate change, conflict resolution, and economic growth increases.

Equality in global decision-making is rooted in sovereignty and the right to self-determination. The United Nations, a prominent global organization, recognizes the equal rights of states to participate in decision-making processes. The General Assembly, a paramount example, assigns each UN member state a single vote, epitomizing that larger and more powerful nation should not unduly sway global community decisions.

The implications of voting equality ripple across numerous dimensions. Firstly, this approach fosters inclusivity and diversity in global decision-making, enabling smaller and less economically potent nations to voice their concerns and engage in shaping global policies. The amalgamation of diverse perspectives enriches the discourse and paves the way for more comprehensive and effective solutions.

Secondly, voting equality ensures equitable distribution of benefits and burdens in global challenges. Decisions forged without voting equality might disproportionately burden specific nations while privileging others. This balance ensures policies that resonate with fairness and long-term sustainability, benefitting all nations collectively.

Thirdly, voting equality contributes to the reinforcement of international law and norms. By adhering to the principles of voting equality, international norms and laws gain authenticity and are more likely to be respected and followed by states. This dynamic strengthens the broader fabric of global governance and cooperation.

However, challenges and critiques cast a shadow on voting equality. Despite the theoretical premise, power imbalances between nations persist, exerting informal influence on decisions. Powerful nations might employ lobbying, financial aid, or diplomatic networks to undermine the true essence of equality subtly. Consequently, the pursuit of consensus among a heterogeneous group of nations becomes a formidable collective action problem, where the interests of some nations may eclipse global common goods, leading to a deadlock or diluted resolutions.

Furthermore, the composition of decision-making bodies might need to accurately reflect the contemporary global power distribution, sidelining emerging economies and marginalized regions. Additionally, resource disparities can hamstring smaller nations, limiting their ability to participate in global decision-making actively. In this context, their equal voting rights might carry less weight in the face of practical challenges.

Moreover, concerns about national sovereignty can cast a pall over the notion of global decision-making. Powerful nations may interpret international cooperation as an infringement on their sovereignty, engendering resistance and non-cooperation, thus impeding progress on pressing global issues.

In order to promote voting equality and, by extension, global equality, various strategies can be employed. The reform of existing structures within global organizations stands as a paramount initiative. The United Nations, for instance, should undertake regular assessments and reforms to align decision-making structures with contemporary geopolitical realities. This might necessitate adjusting voting power, amplifying the representation of emerging economies, and enhancing transparency in decision-making processes.

Capacity building is another avenue for nurturing voting equality. Global institutions could support smaller and less developed nations to enhance their capabilities for effective engagement in global decision-making. This support could manifest as technical assistance, training programs, and allocation of resources to empower these nations to participate more assertively.

Strengthening multilateral diplomacy remains pivotal. Through open dialogues, negotiations, and cooperative efforts, nations can overcome power imbalances and forge a consensus that advances the common good. Multilateral diplomacy also underlines the significance of compromise and the need to accommodate diverse perspectives.

Encouraging civic engagement on the global stage can invigorate the commitment of governments to prioritize global issues. A citizenry well-informed about the implications of global decisions can exert pressure on governments to consider the broader international consequences of their actions, thus amplifying the push for voting equality.

Finally, an emphasis on global education can cultivate a populace that comprehends the value of global cooperation and the role of voting equality in achieving equality among nations. A well-educated citizenry is better equipped to navigate the complexities of global governance, propelling the mission for voting equality forward.

In conclusion, the world's interconnectedness underscores the profound importance of voting equality in global decision-making processes. Although challenges such as power imbalances and resource disparities persist, the principles of inclusivity, fairness, and mutual benefit underscore the necessity of upholding voting equality. Humanity can progress towards a more equitable and just global order by reforming existing structures, promoting capacity building, strengthening multilateral diplomacy, encouraging civic engagement, and enhancing global education. In a landscape defined by intricate challenges, transcending national boundaries, the nurturing of voting equality remains a linchpin in fostering equality among nations and steering the world toward a sustainable and prosperous future for all.

ADDRESSING IMPEDIMENTS TO EQUAL VOTING REPRESENTATION

Equal voting representation is a fundamental tenet in the quest for a fair and just international order. However, reaching this goal is still challenging because of multiple obstacles to equal voting participation in various decision-making venues. By eliminating the complexities that prevent equal voting participation, we may create a world in which each country's voice matters and influences the course of mankind.

Power Dynamics and Geopolitical Realities

Power dynamics and geopolitical realities greatly shadow the goal of equal vote representation within the complex web of global governance. Rather than mirroring the intricacies of the contemporary global landscape, the intricate structures of international organizations such as the United Nations (UN) or the World Trade Organization (WTO) often replicate historical reverberations and economic dominance. This complex dance of power obscures the core of equal representation, and the voices of less powerful nations are consigned to the margins.

In this global theater, the stage is often set by powerful nations' historical legacies and economic prowess. The distribution of voting power is akin to a historical inheritance, where those who held sway in the past continue to wield disproportionate influence in shaping present-day decisions. While grounded in the realities of yesteryears, such a system fails to account for the shifting tides of progress and evolution.

The glaring disparity between major powers and their lesser counterparts creates a dissonance between representation and reality. The voices of smaller nations, with unique perspectives and varied challenges, are muffled in the face of the symphony played by larger, more influential nations. The outcome is an orchestra dominated by a select few, with the harmonious balance of equal representation relegated to a mere backdrop.

Perhaps this is more evident than in the hallowed chambers of the UN Security Council. A chamber that wields the power to shape the fate of nations, its structure often thwarts the aspirations of the many in favor of the privileged few. The perpetual veto power of permanent members, while a relic of post-World War II geopolitics, erects barriers that hinder the emergence of a truly inclusive global order. This elite club often steers key decisions, far-reaching and impactful, leaving the vision of equal voting representation enshrined in the UN's charter teetering on the edge of disillusionment.

The imbalance, while embedded in the fabric of these institutions, is a testament to the profound challenges that equal voting representation faces. It is an indictment of a world order that struggles to evolve beyond the footprints of history. The repercussions reverberate through diplomatic corridors and negotiation tables, where the aspirations of nations, irrespective of size or power, strive to find resonance.

The quest for equitable vote representation remains a steadfast goal in this complex interplay of power. It demands a resetting of the scales, a change that acknowledges the changing dynamics of the world and welcomes a chorus where each nation's voice is valid and cherished. The path toward a society where equitable representation is not just a far-off fantasy but a living, breathing reality begins with transcending the tyranny of historical legacies and economic might. It's a journey that challenges the status quo, reshapes the narratives of power, and weaves a narrative where the symphony of voices resonates in harmony, crafting a new symphony of global governance.

Economic Disparities and Limited Resources

Economic inequalities throw a looming shadow in the complex theater of international decision-making, offering a tremendous barrier to the fulfillment of equal vote participation. The spotlight frequently favors those with economic clout on the stage where nations congregate to discuss and choose the future of the globe. Developing countries need help with the limitations of scarce resources, which limits their capacity to participate effectively in these forums. The result is a story of uneven involvement, in which the resonance of the wealthy drowns out the voices of those fighting to stay up.

In this global arena, attending international conferences, negotiating treaties, and participating in multilateral dialogues require more than intellectual prowess – they demand financial and technical resources that often lie beyond the reach of developing nations. The cost of participation in these discussions extends beyond travel expenses; it encompasses the deployment of expertise, access to information, and the capacity to maneuver through the complex labyrinth of international diplomacy. As developing nations grapple with the intricate jigsaw puzzle of limited resources, their seats at the table are, by default, disadvantaged.

This financial chasm perpetuates a cycle of unequal representation. Developed nations, equipped with robust economies and ample resources, waltz through the complex choreography of international negotiations with relative ease. The corridors of influence are more accessible, and the engagement mechanisms are more navigable. The consequence is a symphony of voices that, while distinct, often harmonize along economic lines, distorting the principle of equal voting representation.

The repercussions of this economic discrepancy resonate far beyond mere participation. A world that pivots on the fulcrum of economic prowess nurtures a culture where the power to shape global narratives is linked to the strength of one's currency. This perpetuates a cycle where the economically powerful continue to wield disproportionate influence, their decisions echoing in corridors of power. Meanwhile, the voices of nations striving to bridge the economic divide are muted, their aspirations held hostage by the weight of their economic constraints.

To dismantle this cycle is to embark on a journey of empowerment. It is to recognize that equal voting representation must transcend economic barriers, embracing the diversity of perspectives that enrich the global discourse. Strategies that level the playing field, such as resource allocation and technical support for developing nations, become instrumental in reshaping the narrative. As these measures take root, a new symphony of voices can emerge, harmonizing across economic lines and resonating with the principle that all nations, regardless of their economic stature, hold an indispensable role in shaping global destiny.

In this pursuit, the world stands on the threshold of transformation – a transformation that bridges the economic chasm and empowers nations to participate on equal footing. As the echo of unequal resources fades and the chorus of diverse voices swells, the world inches closer to the symphony of equal voting representation, a harmonious tapestry woven with the threads of shared destiny and collective aspirations.

Complexities of Cultural Diversity and Languages

The complexities of cultural diversity and languages are a profound impediment to realizing equal voting representation. The grand theater of international discourse aims to weave together the myriad threads of cultures, languages, and perspectives, yet within this intricate tapestry lies a challenge that often goes unnoticed – the dominance of a few languages and the cultural barriers they unintentionally erect.

Global institutions strive to serve as a microcosm of humanity, representing the rich tapestry of cultures that define our world. However, the linguistic landscape is often tilted in favor of a select few, with languages like English emerging as communication conduits. While serving as a lingua franca, this linguistic monopoly inadvertently marginalizes non-English-speaking nations, their voices muted in a chorus dominated by a single tongue. This imbalance disrupts the harmony of equal representation, erecting barriers that hinder the articulation of perspectives.

The challenge extends beyond mere communication; it delves into cultural nuances that define national identities. When nations gather to deliberate and shape the global narrative, the complexities of cultural differences can often be lost in translation. The subtleties that make a point profound or a sentiment profound can dissipate, leading to misunderstandings that permeate negotiations and decision-making processes.

This linguistic and cultural labyrinth often leaves nations needing help to voice their viewpoints effectively. As the world converges to discuss crucial matters, some nations grapple to articulate their stances. Consequently, equal voting representation becomes an idealistic aspiration rather than a tangible reality.

To navigate these complexities is to recognize that representation must extend beyond language. It involves elevating cultural diversity as a cornerstone, acknowledging that each voice, irrespective of its linguistic origin, carries unique insights and experiences. It involves adopting strategies that bridge the linguistic gap, such as enhanced translation services and efforts to promote multilingualism within global institutions.

Moreover, the recognition of cultural nuances must take center stage. Efforts to ensure that translations preserve the essence of each nation's perspective are pivotal. This can be achieved through cross-cultural training, fostering a deeper understanding of cultural contexts among diplomats and negotiators.

In transcending these linguistic and cultural barriers, the global stage can amplify the principle of equal voting representation. It can resonate with many voices, each contributing a distinct hue to the global canvas. As these barriers are dismantled, the world inches closer to a symphony where linguistic diversity and cultural richness harmonize, affirming that all nations, regardless of their languages or cultural contexts, hold a place of significance in shaping humanity's collective destiny.

The journey is complex, requiring a reimagining of communication and negotiation processes. Yet, within this complexity lies the true potential for transformation. This transformation celebrates the mosaic of voices that define our world and resonates with the symphony of equal voting representation, a harmony where diversity and equality intertwine in perfect resonance.

Lack of Civic Awareness and Political Will

The lack of civic awareness and political will within nations is a formidable barrier to equal voting representation. In the theater of international discourse, where nations convene to chart the course of our shared destiny, the absence of informed citizenry and resolute political intent casts a shadow over the pursuit of fairness and equity.

In many corners of the world, citizens need to be made aware of the intricacies and implications of decisions made on the global stage. The grand narratives of international cooperation and equal representation often elude their grasp, creating a chasm between their understanding and the actions of their governments. This disconnect dilutes the urgency of championing equal voting representation, relegating it to the periphery of public consciousness.

Furthermore, the political will to advocate for equal voting representation can falter amidst the clamor of domestic priorities. Governments, ensnared in the web of immediate concerns and competing demands, may need to catch up on the broader context. The allure of short-term gains and political expedience can overshadow the imperative of nurturing a just global order. This discord between the long-term vision of global equity and the immediacy of domestic concerns creates a conundrum that hinders the resonance of equal voting representation.

To navigate this uncharted terrain is to embark on a journey of education and transformation. It calls for a concerted effort to elevate global understanding among citizens, bridging the gap between the decisions of the world stage and their everyday lives. Equipping citizens with the knowledge of the impact of international decisions can elevate the demand for equal voting representation, infusing it with the weight of public support.

Simultaneously, nurturing political will necessitates a recalibration of priorities. Governments must recognize that pursuing global equity is not a distant ideal but a vital cornerstone of their responsibilities. This recognition demands a delicate balancing act, where the urgent and the essential align, paving the way for resolute advocacy for equal representation.

In this transformation journey, nations stand at a crossroads where civic awareness and political will converge. As awareness spreads and political intent aligns, the pursuit of equal voting representation gains momentum. It becomes a shared endeavor that transcends borders and resonates with people's aspirations worldwide.

As the world seeks to overcome this barrier, the path ahead requires unity of purpose and a commitment to change. By fostering civic awareness, governments can harness the power of informed citizenry to propel the demand for equal voting representation. By nurturing political will, they can ensure this demand finds resonance within the hallowed halls of decision-making.

The journey is not without challenges, but it is within these challenges that the potential for transformation lies. As the gap between citizens and global decisions narrows and political intent aligns with the pursuit of equity, the stage is set for a harmonious symphony of voices that collectively shape the course of our shared world. In this world, the principle of equal voting representation resonates as an aspiration and a lived reality.

Strategies for Overcoming Impediments

Addressing these impediments necessitates a multifaceted approach that acknowledges the complexity of the global landscape. To achieve equal voting representation, several strategies can be employed:

1. Reform and Restructuring: Global institutions must undergo reforms that reflect contemporary geopolitical realities. The UN Security Council, for instance, could be expanded to include more diverse representation, reducing the concentration of power among a few permanent members.

2. Resource Allocation: Developed nations could contribute to a fund that supports developing nations' participation in global decision-making processes. This fund could provide financial resources and technical assistance, leveling the playing field and enhancing equal representation.

3. Linguistic Inclusivity: Global institutions should prioritize linguistic inclusivity by providing translation and interpretation services for multiple languages. This approach would facilitate effective communication, enabling all nations to discuss without language barriers.

4. Global Education: Promoting global education within nations can create an informed citizenry that understands the significance of equal voting representation. This awareness can translate into greater pressure on governments to champion equitable representation in international forums.

5. Diplomatic Outreach: Diplomatic efforts should focus on building bridges between nations, fostering understanding, and amplifying the importance of equal representation. Open dialogues and collaborative initiatives can help overcome power imbalances and lead to more equitable outcomes.

6. Public Engagement: Civil society organizations, media outlets, and social platforms can play a vital role in raising awareness about the importance of equal voting representation. Engaging citizens in discussions about global issues can create a groundswell of support for equitable representation.

Equal voting representation is indispensable for fostering a just and equitable global order. The impediments that thwart this principle, such as power dynamics, economic disparities, cultural complexities, and civic apathy, are intricate and interconnected. The international community can address these challenges head-on by employing strategies encompassing institutional reform, resource allocation, linguistic inclusivity, global education, diplomatic outreach, and public engagement.

The journey toward equal voting representation requires collective determination and sustained efforts. As we strive to create a world where every nation's voice carries weight, we must remain vigilant in our pursuit of justice and equity. By transcending the barriers that hinder equal voting representation, we can reshape the global landscape and forge a path toward a future defined by inclusivity, fairness, and the genuine empowerment of all nations.

CHAPTER SEVEN

ENVIRONMENTAL JUSTICE AND GLOBAL RESPONSIBILITY

Environmental Justice and Global Responsibility intertwine as the fundamental pillars of our collective duty to safeguard the planet and its inhabitants. Environmental justice encapsulates the principle that all individuals, regardless of background, should enjoy the same degree of protection from environmental hazards and access to natural resources. It illuminates the inequities that disproportionately burden marginalized communities with pollution, degraded ecosystems, and compromised health. By addressing these disparities, environmental justice strives to create a harmonious coexistence between humanity and its surroundings, fostering a world where each voice is heard and each life cherished.

On a broader canvas, Global Responsibility encompasses the recognition that the Earth's ecological challenges transcend national boundaries. It acknowledges that our actions reverberate globally, underscoring our duty to preserve the environment for present and future generations. Global Responsibility urges nations and individuals to collaborate in cultivating sustainable practices, mitigating climate change, conserving biodiversity, and respecting indigenous knowledge. It's an ethos that underscores the interdependence of all life forms and encourages us to transcend self-interest in favor of a shared destiny.

Environmental Justice and Global Responsibility form the bedrock of a holistic approach to planetary well-being. They beckon us to realign our values, policies, and behaviors to create a world where fairness and sustainability prevail. By addressing disparities at local levels and embracing our interconnectedness on a global scale, we can usher in an era where environmental harmony and human dignity flourish hand in hand. Only through upholding both principles can we aspire to mend the fractures in our ecosystems, mend the fabric of society, and pave the way toward a balanced and prosperous future for all.

THE ENVIRONMENTAL IMPACTS OF GLOBAL DISPARITIES

In an era marked by the ever-deepening threads of trade, technology, and communication that weave our global tapestry, a sobering truth emerges the persistence of global disparities across numerous spheres. While conversations about economic and social inequalities frequently take center stage, a subtler but equally profound facet lies in the shadows—the intricate environmental reverberations of these disparities. Amid the complexities of our interconnected world, one undeniable reality becomes clear: the environment remains unburdened by the constraints of geopolitical borders. It's a force that effortlessly transcends the boundaries of nations and continents, casting its influence far and wide, touching the lives of every individual. As we navigate the twists and turns of our shared journey, the often-overlooked interplay between global disparities and their environmental consequences beckons us to delve deeper.

Beyond the visible threads of economic and social imbalances, a complex tapestry is woven—a tapestry is woven with the environmental threads of interconnectedness, vulnerability, and responsibility. Let us embark on this journey of understanding, navigating the nuanced landscape of how disparities and environmental dynamics collide, shaping the world we inhabit and the legacy we leave for generations.

The Nexus of Disparities and Environmental Strain

One must embark on a journey that uncovers the hidden threads binding them together to fathom the intricate choreography between global disparities and the environment. This intricate tapestry reveals a symphony of cause and effect, where poverty, unequal resource access, limited education, and healthcare disparities intertwine to create a cycle of vulnerability that ensnares marginalized communities. Already teetering on the edge of societal fringes, these communities find themselves at the epicenter of environmental degradation, bearing the brunt of its burdens.

The nexus comes alive when we explore the harsh reality that environmental degradation is unequal. Instead, it gravitates towards those already shackled by economic hardship. Toxic waste sites cast long shadows over neighborhoods devoid of political influence, while pollution hotspots silently poison the air that residents must inhale. Resource extraction zones, engines of economic growth for some, emerge as ecological battlegrounds for others, stripping these communities of their natural heritage and further entrenching their vulnerability.

Imagine the stark juxtaposition of towering urban centers and the sprawling slums that often nestle in their shadows. This paradox is vividly exemplified in many developing nations, where the tide of urbanization has surged ahead, leaving infrastructure development trailing in its wake. The result: informal settlements devoid of necessities. Clean water and sanitation become luxuries, while waste disposal systems remain elusive dreams. These disparities magnify the environmental quandaries. Overburdened landfills spill their contents, contaminating both the earth and groundwater. Contaminated water bodies weave a silent web of health risks, while the air, heavy with pollutants, becomes a silent assailant. Amidst these challenges, the inhabitants endure heightened health risks and the stifling grip of diminished productivity and limited economic opportunities.

The complex interplay of inequalities and environmental stress shapes a gloomy story. It highlights the complicated and self-reinforcing cycle that may be created when societal injustices lead to environmental vulnerability. The possibility for metamorphosis exists, nonetheless, inside the chiaroscuro of this story. We may stop this cycle by severing the links that bind inequities and creating communities that grow in symbiotic harmony with their surroundings. Here we reveal both the difficulties and the potential that arise from the intersection of environmental dynamics and global inequities, and this is where the journey of comprehension starts.

Environmental Refugees and the Global Landscape

The intertwining saga of global disparities and the environment unfurls beyond the confines of local territories, reaching far across continents and hemispheres. Climate change, largely fueled by the actions of industrialized nations, transcends borders to inflict its gravest consequences on regions that have contributed the least to its creation. This alarming phenomenon casts a long shadow over vulnerable communities, compelling them to confront a new reality: that of becoming environmental refugees.

The impacts of climate change ripple across the global landscape, manifesting in the upheaval of entire communities. As sea levels surge, coastal settlements—often inhabited by the economically marginalized—find themselves engulfed by the very waters that once sustained them. Unpredictable and extreme weather events wreak havoc, dislodging populations from their ancestral homes. Changing agricultural patterns, a response to shifting climates, disrupt long-standing food security, driving populations to migrate for sustenance.

The result is a heartbreaking narrative of environmental refugees—individuals and families forced to abandon their homes due to environmental degradation. This heartrending plight is inextricably linked to the overarching canvas of global disparities. The very communities that have contributed least to environmental degradation find themselves grappling with its most devastating consequences. This bitter irony lays bare the deep-seated injustices of our world.

Consider the vivid microcosm of vulnerability found in the Pacific Islands. Places like Tuvalu and Kiribati, picturesque archipelagos, are precariously perched in the path of rising sea levels. These nations emit minuscule amounts of greenhouse gases, making them virtually negligible contributors to climate change. Yet, they stand at the precipice of existential crisis. The rising tides threaten their land and their very way of life. Coastal erosion, salinization of freshwater sources, and the specter of inundation cast dark shadows over these island nations.

The discrepancy in the capacity to adapt and mitigate presents a painful paradox. Wealthier nations, often the prime culprits in the climate crisis, possess the resources to erect fortifications against encroaching seas and to implement climate-resilient technologies. In stark contrast, nations like Tuvalu and Kiribati grapple with limited resources, rendering their fight for survival an uphill battle. The burden of adaptation, wrought by environmental changes spurred by disparities, is unevenly distributed, reflecting a world fraught with inequalities.

The unfolding saga of environmental refugees casts a glaring light on the multifaceted nature of global disparities. Beyond economic inequality, these disparities materialize in resilience, adaptation, and the capacity to withstand the impacts of a changing world. The tale of environmental refugees becomes a poignant reminder that the global tapestry is woven with threads of privilege and disadvantage, where the choices of a few can ripple catastrophically across the lives of many.

An urgent call to action resounds within the poignant narratives of those dislocated by environmental turmoil. The journey ahead necessitates more than environmental stewardship; it entails a thorough reexamination of the social frameworks that sustain disparities. It urges us to confront the underlying factors that make certain communities more susceptible to environmental shifts than others. In acknowledging the intricate interplay of these challenges, we forge a path toward a fairer world.

Global Responsibility and Environmental Stewardship

Global responsibility stands out as a guiding concept in the maze of difficulties. Rich countries and international organizations must adhere to this philosophy to fulfill their moral obligation to address the effects of inequalities on the environment. This dedication necessitates actions that go beyond national boundaries and self-interest, casting a larger net of stewardship over the well-being of our world.

In this realm of responsibility, initiatives like climate financing, technology transfer, and capacity building stand as bridges, spanning the chasm between nations of varying resources. By providing financial support to vulnerable regions, sharing technological advancements, and enhancing the skills of local communities, these actions embody the spirit of global responsibility. It is a recognition that environmental challenges are universal, and the privilege of affluence comes with the weighty obligation to extend a helping hand.

Furthermore, at the heart of this principle lies the essential task of incorporating indigenous wisdom and local voices into decision-making processes. By doing so, environmental interventions gain a depth of understanding rooted in the intricate relationship between communities and their surroundings. This synergy bolsters the efficacy of such interventions and nurtures a sense of ownership and empowerment within these communities.

The REDD+ program—Reducing Emissions from Deforestation and Forest Degradation- is a striking illustration of this principle in action. Designed to curb deforestation in developing nations, this initiative aligns with global climate goals and addresses the social and economic disparities that often underlie environmental challenges. By recognizing the pivotal role of forests in climate regulation and the livelihoods of local populations, REDD+ intertwines environmental conservation with poverty alleviation. This intersection is a testament to the potential of aligning environmental and societal objectives.

Essentially, the principle of global responsibility underscores the symbiotic relationship between nations and the environment. It emphasizes that the choices of the privileged hold the power to uplift or oppress and that these choices ripple across our shared global ecosystem. By heeding this call, we set forth on a transformative journey that transcends borders and spans generations, nurturing a world where the privileged extend their hand in stewardship, where disparities dissolve, and where environmental well-being is a collective commitment.

Environmental Diplomacy: Shaping Global Relations

The environment has a dual function in the complex web of international interactions, serving as both a battleground and a conduit to create a narrative that transcends geopolitical boundaries and fosters cooperation. Resource disputes can potentially escalate into major geopolitical conflict in this dynamically interplaying world. Still, environmental problems can also serve as strong unifying forces that push nations to cooperate on common solutions.

At the heart of this dichotomy lies the intrinsic value of environmental diplomacy—a diplomatic approach that seeks to address environmental issues through negotiations, treaties, and cooperative agreements. Recognizing that environmental problems transcend borders underscores the importance of building bridges for mutual benefit rather than erecting barriers of discord.

Disputes over vital resources, be it water or energy, exemplify the potential for environmental issues to escalate into international conflicts. As water scarcity intensifies and energy demands surge, nations are entangled in disputes that transcend their borders. These conflicts cast ripples extending far beyond their origin, affecting neighboring countries and disrupting global equilibrium.

Conversely, environmental diplomacy holds the promise of transforming conflicts into cooperative endeavors. Shared environmental challenges can propel nations to transcend their differences and pool resources toward common goals. This shared pursuit of sustainability breeds cooperation, steering nations toward more comprehensive and enduring solutions.

One striking illustration of this transformative potential lies in the story of the Aral Sea catastrophe. Once a flourishing inland sea, it fell victim to water diversion for agricultural purposes, resulting in a dramatic shrinkage. The environmental fallout devastated ecosystems, triggered health crises and inflicted economic losses upon nations like Uzbekistan and Kazakhstan. The shrinking sea even led to conflicts over dwindling resources.

However, amidst the devastation, a ray of hope emerged through environmental diplomacy. Collaborative efforts between the affected nations and international support have yielded remarkable strides in restoring the Aral Sea's ecosystem and mitigating its consequences. This restoration project stands as a testament to the capacity of environmental diplomacy to transcend disparities and cultivate cooperative solutions. It reveals how shared environmental concerns can transcend political differences, forging a path toward healing and resilience.

Environmental diplomacy, while challenging, holds the promise of recalibrating global relations. It recognizes that the environment is a shared legacy—a resource that transcends national sovereignty. By fostering cooperation and dialogue, it offers a means to navigate complex environmental issues in a way that safeguards our planet's future and strengthens the bonds between nations.

As we journey through the landscape of international relations, we find environmental diplomacy a potent tool to reshape narratives of discord into tales of collaboration. It is an invitation to craft a new narrative where the environment, rather than being a source of conflict, becomes a bridge that unites nations in pursuing a sustainable and harmonious future.

The Power of Environmental Education and Empowerment

Addressing global disparities necessitates a long-term perspective that encompasses education and empowerment. Environmental literacy equips communities with the knowledge to advocate for their rights, make sustainable choices, and hold governments and industries accountable.

In the bustling streets of Nairobi's Kibera slum, an innovative project took root: the Kibera School for Girls. This institution not only imparts education but also instills environmental consciousness. Students learn about waste management, sustainable agriculture, and clean energy. They become change agents within their families and communities, altering mindsets and catalyzing positive change. This example underscores the transformative potential of education in breaking the cycle of disparities and fostering environmental stewardship.

The threads of global disparities and environmental impacts are tightly woven. While these interactions often reflect an unjust reality, they offer a canvas for change. The global community stands at a crossroads—faced with perpetuating inequity or cultivating a harmonious convergence.

The path forward requires a symphony of efforts: equitable resource distribution, technological innovation, policy reform, international cooperation, and environmental education. We can only curtail the environmental degradation that perpetuates them by addressing global disparities. Simultaneously, by championing environmental sustainability, we can mitigate the disproportionate impacts of these disparities and create a world where nations thrive in ecological harmony.

Ultimately, the quest for balance beckons us to transcend borders and divisions. It calls upon us to embrace our shared responsibility as custodians of the Earth, recognizing that environmental impacts mirror our collective choices. By crafting a narrative that intertwines social equity and environmental well-being, we can redefine the global landscape where disparities dissipate, and the environment flourishes as a common legacy.

CREATING A LEVEL-PLAYING FIELD FOR ENVIRONMENTAL RESPONSIBILITY

The imperative to create a level playing field for environmental responsibility transcends national borders. As humanity grapples with climate change, resource depletion, and ecological degradation, the need for joint efforts among nations becomes paramount. By embracing shared goals and equitable strategies, nations can pave the way for a sustainable future that reflects the principles of unity, fairness, and prosperity for all.

Environmental responsibility is no longer confined to national jurisdictions; it is a global challenge that requires collective action. As nations industrialize and urbanize, they contribute to greenhouse gas emissions, pollution, and resource exploitation that have far-reaching impacts. These effects are not evenly distributed, often hitting vulnerable nations harder and exacerbating existing inequalities. Therefore, a level playing field for environmental responsibility necessitates joint efforts to mitigate the effects and ensure equal participation in creating a sustainable world.

In pursuing environmental responsibility, it is essential to recognize the inherent inequalities among nations. Developed nations have historically been major contributors to environmental degradation, benefiting from industrialization and unchecked resource consumption. On the other hand, developing nations face challenges such as poverty, limited access to technology, and inadequate infrastructure. This dichotomy underscores the urgency of creating an equitable framework that accommodates nations' diverse capabilities and circumstances.

Joint Contributions for Equality and Peaceful Environment:
Establishing global targets and commitments forms the cornerstone of collaborative environmental responsibility. Agreements like the Paris Agreement aim to limit global temperature rise and promote sustainable development. Such agreements demonstrate a shared understanding of the urgency and responsibility to address environmental issues collectively.

Developed nations can create a level playing field by facilitating technology transfer and capacity-building initiatives. By sharing advanced green technologies with developing nations, they can bridge the technological gap and enable these countries to leapfrog into cleaner, more sustainable practices.

Collaboration can extend to equitable resource management. Developed nations can invest in sustainable practices that ensure resource availability, while developing nations can adopt responsible resource utilization to prevent depletion and environmental degradation.

Developed nations can contribute to environmental equality by providing climate financing to developing nations. This financial support can aid in mitigation, adaptation, and fostering sustainable development in regions vulnerable to climate impacts. Collaboration for biodiversity conservation is vital for a peaceful environment. Nations can work together to establish protected areas, share conservation best practices, and combat illegal wildlife trade, safeguarding the Earth's rich biological heritage for future generations.

Joint efforts to promote knowledge exchange and environmental education can empower nations to make informed decisions. By sharing experiences, research, and best practices, nations can create a harmonious environment where equal knowledge underpins responsible actions.

Overcoming Challenges to Equality in Environmental Responsibility:

Economic inequalities can hinder collaboration on environmental responsibility. Addressing this requires developed nations to provide financial assistance and incentives to help developing nations transition to sustainable practices without compromising their development goals.

Different nations have varying priorities, and reconciling these differences is a challenge. Diplomacy and international negotiations must focus on finding common ground and showcasing the interconnectedness of environmental issues with other global concerns.

Achieving policy alignment among diverse nations is complex. International platforms and forums should encourage open dialogue and negotiation, fostering an understanding of each nation's unique circumstances and facilitating policy harmonization. Environmental responsibility demands sustained commitment. Nations must continually invest in collaboration, acknowledging that short-term gains must maintain the long-term goal of environmental sustainability and equality.

Creating a level playing field for environmental responsibility is not just a moral imperative but an essential step toward ensuring a peaceful and prosperous world for all nations. Collaborative efforts based on shared goals, equitable strategies, and mutual respect can transcend national interests and forge a path to global sustainability. By addressing inequalities, sharing resources, and leveraging technology, nations can work in unison to mitigate climate change, conserve biodiversity, and promote responsible resource management.

The journey is not without challenges, but through diplomacy, education, and a commitment to future generations, nations can collaboratively build a world where environmental responsibility is a shared foundation for equality and peace. As the sun sets on this discussion, the dawn of a united and sustainable future awaits, guided by the principles of collaboration, harmony, and shared responsibility.

THE ROLE OF INTERNATIONAL AGREEMENTS IN ENVIRONMENTAL EQUITY

The importance of international accords in advancing environmental fairness has grown in a world of interconnected ecosystems and common environmental problems. In order to solve urgent environmental challenges, these agreements act as bridges that unite nations across borders and cut beyond political and economic interests.

Environmental equity is rooted in the recognition that the consequences of environmental degradation are not uniformly distributed. While the impacts of climate change, pollution, and resource depletion are felt globally, vulnerable and marginalized communities often bear a disproportionate burden. This inequity reflects broader societal disparities and underscores the need for a collaborative framework that rectifies these imbalances.

International agreements play a pivotal role in addressing environmental inequities by establishing shared goals, principles, and strategies that guide global environmental actions. These agreements provide a platform for nations to come together, irrespective of their political, economic, or historical differences, and collectively work towards sustainable solutions.

At the heart of international agreements lie shared commitments that bind nations to a common environmental agenda. Notably among these is the Paris Agreement, a pivotal accord designed to curb the escalation of global temperatures and alleviate the repercussions of climate change. This agreement embodies the tenets of ecological fairness by acknowledging historical imbalances and urging developed nations, which have played a substantial role in carbon emissions, to shoulder more significant responsibilities in mitigating their environmental influence.

One of the cornerstones of environmental equity is the transfer of clean technologies and capacity-building initiatives from developed to developing nations. This transfer narrows the technological gap, enabling developing nations to leapfrog into sustainable practices. International agreements facilitate this exchange by creating a supportive technology-sharing framework, promoting cooperation that transcends geopolitical divides.

International agreements also address the financial aspect of environmental equity. The Green Climate Fund, established under the United Nations Framework Convention on Climate Change, exemplifies this approach.

This fund, designed to support low-income countries in addressing and adapting to the impacts of climate change, relies on contributions from more affluent nations. This financial framework promotes equitable development and ensures that vulnerable nations possess the essential resources to confront environmental issues.

International agreements contribute to environmental equity by emphasizing the preservation of biodiversity and the establishment of protected areas. The Convention on Biological Diversity fosters collaboration in safeguarding the planet's rich biological heritage. It recognizes that biodiversity loss affects all nations and encourages collective efforts to conserve ecosystems that sustain life on Earth.

While international agreements hold immense potential for promoting environmental equity, challenges persist. Political tensions, varying national priorities, and the implementation gap pose hurdles to effective cooperation. Overcoming these challenges requires a steadfast commitment to diplomatic negotiations, transparency, and accountability.

In the future, international agreements must evolve to address emerging environmental challenges. As the world grapples with issues like plastic pollution, deforestation, and loss of freshwater resources, agreements must adapt to reflect these concerns and foster equitable solutions.

International agreements function as the threads connecting nations within the fabric of global environmental endeavors, working towards establishing a sustainable and equitable future. These accords acknowledge the interdependence of environmental issues and that everyone must address them. International agreements pave the way for environmental fairness through fostering shared commitments, technology transfer, finance for equitable development, and biodiversity preservation.

As we navigate an ever-changing world, the role of international agreements in promoting environmental equity remains pivotal. The path forward demands collaborative efforts, diplomatic perseverance, and a commitment to justice. Only through such concerted action can we ensure that every nation, regardless of its past contributions or economic standing, has an equal opportunity to shape a greener, fairer, and more harmonious global environment—one where the principles of equity and sustainability intertwine to shape a better future for all.

SUSTAINABILITY AND COLLABORATION: CHARTING A SUSTAINABLE FUTURE

The urgent need to achieve sustainability and foster teamwork for a common future has taken on unprecedented importance during complex environmental challenges. The intricate interplay of interconnected ecological systems, closely intertwined with human activities, underscores the urgent need for a paradigm shift toward sustainable practices.

This all-encompassing exploration delves deep into the intricate landscape of sustainability and collaboration, underscoring how these intertwined concepts hold the key to charting a trajectory toward a sustainable future—ensuring the prosperity of our planet, its inhabitants, and future generations.

Sustainability transcends the conventional notion of environmental conservation; it embodies a holistic approach that encompasses economic prosperity, social equity, and ecological harmony. At its core, sustainability entails addressing present needs while safeguarding the ability of future generations to meet their own needs. Achieving this delicate balance requires conscientious resource management, responsible consumption, and nurturing harmonious relationships between humanity and the natural world.

The path toward sustainability demands collaborative endeavors on a global scale. Environmental challenges recognize no boundaries; the ramifications of pollution generated in one corner of the world reverberate across ecosystems and communities thousands of miles away. Collaboration acts as the bridge connecting nations, industries, and individuals in a shared pursuit of common objectives. It transcends national interests, engendering a collective responsibility toward safeguarding our planet.

Governments play a pivotal role in propelling collaborative sustainability initiatives. They craft policies, regulations, and frameworks guiding industries, businesses, and citizens toward sustainable practices. International agreements, epitomized by the United Nations Sustainable Development Goals (SDGs), provide a roadmap for countries to address issues from poverty eradication to climate action collectively. Diplomatic negotiations and consensus-building enable governments to establish global norms and standards that foster sustainability.

Industries wield considerable influence over environmental impact. While they can contribute to environmental degradation, they also possess the capacity to lead transformative shifts. Collaborative sustainability in the business sector entails adopting eco-friendly technologies, practicing responsible supply chain management, and embracing principles of circular economies. The proliferation of sustainability certifications and voluntary initiatives underscores industries' growing alignment with global sustainability objectives.

Collaborative sustainability extends beyond institutional corridors; it permeates civil society and grassroots movements. From youth-led climate protests to community-driven conservation endeavors, individuals and local communities emerge as pivotal advocates for sustainable practices. Civil society collaboration involves knowledge dissemination, awareness campaigns, and collective action to hold governments and industries accountable for their environmental commitments.

Science and innovation catalyze collaborative sustainability efforts. Through interdisciplinary research, technological advancements, and data-driven insights, scientists play a pivotal role in identifying solutions to complex environmental challenges. Collaboration among scientists, policymakers, and industries ensures that evidence-based decisions shape sustainability initiatives. Open-source knowledge sharing facilitates the global diffusion of innovative ideas.

Collaborative sustainability encounters its share of challenges. Competing interests, divergent priorities, and the lack of enforceable mechanisms can impede progress. Overcoming these hurdles necessitates diplomatic negotiations, consensus-building, and an understanding that a sustainable future benefits all. Strengthening international institutions, enhancing transparency, and emphasizing the interconnectedness of global challenges are integral to advancing progress.

Technology serves as a conduit for collaborative sustainability efforts. Digital platforms, data analytics, and communication technologies facilitate the exchange of ideas, information, and best practices across borders. These tools empower nations, organizations, and individuals, fostering knowledge sharing, innovation, and collective problem-solving. Harnessing technological capabilities amplifies the impact of collaborative sustainability endeavors.

Education plays a pivotal role in fostering collaborative sustainability. By nurturing environmental literacy, fostering critical thinking, and instilling a sense of global citizenship, education empowers individuals to shape a sustainable future actively. Curricula emphasizing sustainable practices, ethical consumption, and ecological comprehension provide the foundation for informed decision-making across societal strata.

Collaborative sustainability transcends scales—at local, national, and global levels. Local communities serve as crucial implementers of sustainability initiatives on the ground. National governments align policies with international commitments, while global collaborations catalyze transformative change. The Paris Agreement exemplifies the potency of global cooperation in addressing climate change's dire implications.

Collaboration begets innovation, birthing sustainable technologies, practices, and solutions. Renewable energy technologies, sustainable agricultural methods, and resource conservation strategies arise from collaborative efforts. Innovation extends beyond technological advancements; it encompasses groundbreaking business models, novel financial mechanisms, and policy frameworks that synergize economic prosperity with environmental stewardship.

Collaborative sustainability rests on an ethical imperative—acknowledging the interconnectedness of all life on Earth and the shared duty to safeguard it. Recognizing that environmental degradation disproportionately affects marginalized communities heightens the commitment to collaborate for equitable outcomes. Indigenous knowledge, cultural heritage, and traditional practices enrich the tapestry of collaborative sustainability efforts.

As we navigate the trajectory toward sustainability, collaboration emerges as the guiding force. The formidable challenges—climate change, biodiversity loss, and resource scarcity—demand collective endeavors that transcend political, cultural, and geographic boundaries. The vision is vivid: a world where nations unite to curb carbon emissions, industries adopt circular practices, communities become stewards of ecosystems, and individuals make choices with global resonance.

In this future realm, collaborative sustainability underpins thriving ecosystems, equitable societies, and harmonious coexistence between humanity and nature. It signifies a departure from shortsighted gains toward the collective prosperity of both present and future generations. As individuals, communities, industries, and nations align aspirations, values, and actions with the tenets of collaborative sustainability, they harness a transformative force that redefines progress, nurtures biodiversity, and safeguards the delicate equilibrium of our planet.

In summation, the epoch for collaboration, innovation, and molding a sustainable future is upon us. Every action, decision, and choice resonates in a future where equilibrium prevails, ecosystems rejuvenate, and humanity thrives. Collaborative sustainability is the vessel charting this visionary course that beckons collective action, surmounting barriers and embracing our role as guardians of a precious planet. Now is the time to act, collaborate, and shape a sustainable future.

CHAPTER EIGHT

CULTURAL EXCHANGE AND MUTUAL UNDERSTANDING

Cultural Exchange and Mutual Understanding emerge as potent catalysts for fostering equality among nations in a world distinguished by diversity, where cultures mix and countries intersect in the international arena. At its core, this concept symbolizes the tremendous importance of building relationships, crossing boundaries, and embracing the rich tapestry of human heritage. It represents an effort beyond diplomatic negotiations and economic links, reaching into the heart of what brings us all together as a global community.

Cultural exchange is a dynamic process that enables societies to share their traditions, values, and ways of life; it goes beyond simple surface-level connections. It is the sharing of ideas through language, music, cuisine, and customs as a means of communication across ideological and geographical boundaries. Nations can explore uncharted territory and appreciate various points of view by participating in cultural exchanges.

In this interwoven narrative, the concept of mutual understanding takes center stage. It culminates with active listening, empathetic engagement, and an earnest desire to comprehend one another. By immersing in each other's cultures and narratives, nations can forge a profound connection that transcends the surface and delves into the core of shared humanity. Mutual understanding shatters stereotypes, dispels biases, and lays the groundwork for respect and equality among nations.

Cultural exchange and mutual understanding work in tandem to foster equality among nations by dismantling the barriers that division often erects. They offer a space where appreciation and curiosity flourish, fostering an environment where nations are willing to learn from one another and stand in solidarity. In this narrative, equality isn't just about political negotiations; it's about recognizing the inherent worth of each nation's cultural legacy and affording them respect and consideration.

As we traverse the global landscape, navigating through cultural nuances and intricacies, the journey of cultural exchange and mutual understanding emerges as a pivotal thread in international relations. It embodies the belief that embracing diversity doesn't weaken a nation but strengthens the bonds that connect us all. Through this exchange, nations can build bridges of empathy and cooperation that serve as the foundation for a world where equality prevails, irrespective of size, influence, or economic status.

EMBRACING DIVERSITY AND FOSTERING MUTUAL UNDERSTANDING

Diversity, a hallmark ingrained in the very fabric of our existence, paints a portrait of unparalleled potential. As humanity's narrative unfolds, the coexistence of multifarious cultures, languages, traditions, and histories paints the vibrant tapestry of our shared global landscape. Amid this kaleidoscope of diversity, a challenge beckons: the art of harmonizing the divergent threads that shape us. Within this challenge lies the transformative power of fostering mutual understanding—a cornerstone that, when laid, fortifies the foundation of equality among nations. In this intricate dance of perspectives, the symphony of mutual understanding emerges as a unifying force, threading connections between disparate fragments and weaving the promise of an egalitarian world.

Diversity is abundant wherever you look, from the humming markets of Marrakech, where vivid fabrics communicate tales of years past, to the serene temples of Kyoto, where respectful murmurs reverberate in the recesses of centuries-old buildings. It's embodied in the rhythmic beats of African drums, a heartbeat that resonates across continents, and in the mellifluous strains of European classical compositions that echo the aspirations of generations. It's not confined to the grandeur of landmarks; diversity pulses in the daily interactions, traditions, and conversations that illuminate the lives of people around the globe.

Diversity is an eternal dialogue, a dance where cultures converse, exchange, and intertwine. It's an ever-evolving narrative that finds expression in the flavors of local cuisines, the brushstrokes of indigenous art, and the cadence of native languages. The essence of diversity lies not only in its outward manifestations but also in its power to foster innovation, resilience, and empathy.

When diverse perspectives converge, they birth new ways of thinking, enabling societies to tackle complex challenges from myriad angles. The tapestry of diversity is woven with threads of human resilience, a testament to our ability to adapt, learn, and thrive in a world of change. It's a reminder that every voice matters, every story is significant, and every heritage is a treasure trove of wisdom.

In celebrating diversity, we affirm our commitment to embracing the richness of human identity. We acknowledge that the symphony of cultures contributes to the symposium of humanity—a collective endeavor that resonates far beyond individual borders. From the ancient traditions of indigenous communities to the innovative technologies of modern cities, diversity enkindles progress, reminding us that our shared destiny is intertwined in a global narrative that transcends time and space.

As we navigate the tapestry of diversity, let us not merely coexist but consciously strive to comprehend, appreciate, and celebrate one another's narratives. By doing so, we embrace our shared humanity, acknowledging that within our myriad differences lies a unifying thread of aspirations, dreams, and a collective longing for a world that cherishes and harmonizes the unique notes of every individual's story.

The Bridge of Mutual Understanding

Mutual understanding arises as a transcendent bridge that crosses the chasms of miscommunication and fosters the development of true connections in the great expanse of a diverse world. The guiding light leads us through the complex maze of cultural inconsistencies, language quirks, and contrasting worldviews. The powerful elixir that pushes us past the boundaries of our prejudices and encourages us to embrace the rich tapestry of human experiences that cover our world is mutual understanding.

At its core, mutual understanding represents the profound act of delving into the narratives of others, seeking not only comprehension but also empathy. It entails the deliberate effort to step outside the boundaries of our perspectives, to wander through the landscapes of alternative viewpoints, and to immerse ourselves in the lives of those whose stories diverge from our own. It's a process that requires unraveling preconceived notions and recognizing the legitimacy of other perspectives.

The true potency of mutual understanding lies in its capacity to dismantle the walls erected by misconception and prejudice. It is the force that transforms strangers into allies, fostering a profound sense of kinship and camaraderie. As we embark on this journey of comprehension, we begin to perceive the world through the eyes of others—acknowledging their joys, understanding their struggles, and embracing their aspirations.

Mutual understanding is a balm for a world grappling with division and strife. It is a salve that nurtures the wounds inflicted by misunderstanding and animosity. This bridge's power is revealed when individuals from disparate backgrounds find common ground, bridging the gaps that once seemed insurmountable. It transcends linguistic, cultural, and ideological boundaries, offering a universal language of empathy that resonates across the spectrum of human experience.

On the grand stage of international relations, mutual understanding is the master key that opens doors to cooperation, diplomacy, and the pursuit of global harmony. It's the conduit through which world leaders can engage in meaningful discourse, seeking shared solutions to complex challenges that transcend borders. By truly comprehending the perspectives of other nations, leaders can navigate the intricate diplomatic landscape with wisdom and sensitivity.

Imagine a world where mutual understanding prevails—conflicts are averted, and collaborations flourish. In this realm, diplomacy is marked by the genuine desire to comprehend the needs and aspirations of other nations. It's a space where the seeds of peace are sown, germinating into fruitful relationships that yield shared prosperity and progress.

In the journey towards global harmony, mutual understanding is the compass that guides us through uncharted waters. It's a testament to the resilience of the human spirit, reminding us that our stories, though diverse, are woven with threads of shared emotions, desires, and dreams. As we cross this bridge, we recognize that while our paths may differ, they intersect in the realm of our collective humanity.

The bridge of mutual understanding manifests our innate capacity for empathy and connection. It's a testament to our shared yearning for unity and cohesion in a world of diversity. As we traverse this bridge, we embark on a journey of discovery that leads us to the heart of the human experience, where bonds are forged, horizons are expanded, and the symphony of global harmony finds its resonance.

The Role of World Leaders in Embracing Diversity

World leaders, occupying pivotal positions of influence and authority, are responsible for shaping the global narrative of diversity and mutual understanding. Herein lies the potential to lay the groundwork for equality among nations, regardless of their size, influence, or economic status. But how can world leaders embrace diversity to foster mutual understanding and, in turn, promote equality among nations?

1. Educational Reforms: Education is the cornerstone of transformation. World leaders can introduce comprehensive curricula that educate their citizens about other nations' cultures, histories, and perspectives. By fostering cultural literacy early on, societies can cultivate empathy and curiosity about the world beyond their borders.

2. Cultural Exchange Programs: Initiating and supporting cultural exchange programs can be instrumental in breaking down barriers. World leaders can promote cross-cultural understanding and dispel stereotypes by facilitating opportunities for citizens to experience other cultures firsthand.

3. Promotion of Inclusivity: Embracing diversity requires creating an inclusive environment that celebrates differences. World leaders can enact policies that protect minority rights, ensure representation,

and counter discrimination, fostering respect for all cultures and nations.

4. International Collaboration: World leaders can actively engage in international collaborations encouraging dialogue, cooperation, and problem-solving. Joint efforts on climate change, poverty eradication, and healthcare can foster a sense of shared purpose and understanding.

5. Media and Communication: The media plays a pivotal role in shaping public opinion. World leaders can promote responsible and balanced media coverage that highlights the positive aspects of diverse cultures, counteracting the spread of stereotypes and biases.

6. Cultural Diplomacy: Utilizing cultural diplomacy, world leaders can leverage art, music, literature, and other cultural forms to foster connections between nations. Cultural events, exhibitions, and exchanges can serve as dialogue and mutual understanding platforms.

7. Leadership by Example: World leaders can set an example by championing diversity within their administrations and societies. Appointing individuals from diverse backgrounds to leadership positions sends a powerful message about the value of inclusion.

8. Global Policy Frameworks: International agreements and policies that prioritize diversity and mutual understanding can have far-reaching effects. World leaders can collaborate to develop frameworks that promote cultural exchange, protect indigenous rights, and uphold cultural heritage.

9. Humanitarian Initiatives: Engaging in humanitarian efforts that transcend national boundaries can unite nations in shared

compassion and empathy. Responding to global crises and offering assistance to those in need reinforces the interconnectedness of our world.

10. Public Awareness Campaigns: World leaders can launch campaigns emphasizing the benefits of diversity and mutual understanding. Such campaigns can inspire citizens to seek cross-cultural engagement and exchange opportunities actively.

Equality of Nations: A Consequence of Mutual Understanding

Mutual understanding, often regarded as a means to an end, is a profound transformation in itself—a transformation that blooms into the radiant flower of equality among nations. As the tapestry of global relations intricately interweaves, mutual understanding is the catalyst that unravels hierarchical paradigms, ushering nations into a realm where equality flourishes.

In this realm, mutual understanding becomes more than a bridge—it is the foundation upon which the edifice of equality is constructed. A seismic shift occurs as world leaders recognize the value of embracing diverse perspectives and fostering empathy. The conventional notions of power dynamics and supremacy that often underscore international interactions crumble beneath the weight of understanding.

The heart of this transformation lies in dismantling the illusion that the significance of a nation is proportionate to its size or influence. Mutual understanding proclaims that every nation, irrespective of its physical dimensions, possesses a unique thread that contributes to the grand tapestry of humanity. The rich heritage of a small nation is just as precious as the cultural legacy of a larger one. This revelation challenges the preconceived notions of superiority and inferiority that have long clouded diplomatic engagements.

As mutual understanding thrives, respect blossoms in its wake. Steeped in the wisdom of empathetic comprehension, world leaders grasp that no perspective is inconsequential. No culture is less worthy, and no voice deserves to be silenced. This realization reverberates in the corridors of global politics, transcending linguistic barriers and ideological differences.

The metamorphosis engendered by mutual understanding culminates in tangible policies prioritizing all nations' rights and sovereignty. The small and the mighty, the wealthy and the struggling—all are afforded equal consideration. Equality is no longer a distant aspiration but a living, breathing reality nurtured by a collective commitment to dialogue, cooperation, and the pursuit of global welfare.

Imagine a world where the principles of equality flourish, where nations stand united on a level playing field. Here, equality extends beyond the mere proclamation of ideals—it's a vibrant pulse that underpins the actions of world leaders. Once marred by power imbalances, diplomacy is revitalized by genuine understanding and respect.

In this world, solutions are sought through collaboration rather than coercion. Dialogue supersedes dominance, and consensus replaces confrontation. The pressing global challenges—climate change, poverty, or conflict—become shared endeavors where nations contribute based on their strengths, not their size.

The symphony of equality echoes through every international engagement, harmonizing the diverse voices of nations into a chorus of unity. And as the world watches, mutual understanding continues to blossom, intertwining with the roots of equality and nurturing a future where every nation's sovereignty, human rights, and freedom are not just revered concepts but inviolable truths.

The evolution from mutual understanding to equality is a transformative journey. It's a journey that dismantles hierarchies, amplifies respect, and redefines the dynamics of international relations. As world leaders embrace this journey, they embrace a world where nations, no matter how big or small, stand as equals—bound by empathy, united by dialogue, and guided by the luminous path of mutual understanding.

Diversity is important in human pursuits, and respect for one another orchestrates harmony. World leaders are uniquely positioned to guide their nations toward a period when global equality is a reality rather than an ideal since they are in a position of power. By embracing diversity, promoting understanding, and upholding the rights of every nation, international leaders may leave a legacy that cuts across borders and pave the way for a world unified by shared values and empathy.

CULTURAL DIPLOMACY: A CATALYST FOR HARMONIOUS INTERNATIONAL RELATIONS

The idea of cultural diplomacy is a tremendous force that affects how states interact with one another and resonates as a potential means of achieving international equality. This discourse has developed through time and now encompasses a variety of viewpoints and behaviors that go beyond conventional categories. It is smoothly woven into both cultural policy studies and international relations. The concept of "cultural diplomacy" has evolved beyond its original connotation to encompass a wide range of activities, including involvement with civil society, foreign policy, soft power, and even the advancement of societal well-being. As humanity develops, it becomes clear that cultural diplomacy can open doors for peaceful international relations and achieving global equality among nations.

The traditional notion of cultural diplomacy as a soft power tool wielded by states and international organizations to advance their foreign policy objectives has evolved into a diverse entity that defies clear boundaries. A more expansive perspective has emerged, one that recognizes cultural diplomacy not just as a means to an end but as a substantive policy area in itself. In this paradigm, cultural diplomacy is no longer confined to government diplomats engaging in formal exchanges. Instead, it extends its reach to embrace citizens, civil society actors, artists, and cultural institutions as active participants in forging cross-border connections. This evolution underscores a shift from cultural diplomacy as a tool of statecraft to a vehicle for societal empowerment, economic growth, and social cohesion.

However, even as cultural diplomacy takes on this broader role, it remains a term enveloped in ambivalence. Its blurred boundaries can encompass both genuine efforts to foster international understanding and collaborations, as well as the exploitation of culture for geopolitical or economic gain. This duality underscores the complex interplay between culture, power, and diplomacy in an interconnected world.

The prevailing "methodological nationalism" in policy and scholarship, where the focus largely rests on intergovernmental cultural exchanges, has created gaps in understanding the motivations and contributions of civil society actors and the role of cities in practicing cultural diplomacy. These gaps are crucial in unraveling the true potential of cultural diplomacy as a catalyst for harmonious international relations and equality among nations.

Acknowledging these disparities, a significant workshop was organized at the European University Institute's Robert Schuman Centre for Advanced Studies in Florence. Conducted on 21 May 2019, this workshop signaled a departure from traditional narratives, seeking to explore the previously overlooked facets of cultural diplomacy. This special issue culminates the thought-provoking discussions and insights from that gathering.

At its core, cultural diplomacy transcends the political and economic considerations that often dominate international relations. It operates on a level that resonates with shared humanity, transcending the barriers of language, geography, and ideology. When nations engage in cultural diplomacy, they engage in symbolic gestures and a profound exchange of values, narratives, and aspirations. This exchange forms the bedrock of mutual understanding—a force that bridges the chasm of misunderstanding and lays the groundwork for trust and cooperation.

Furthermore, cultural diplomacy can remarkably empower civil society actors and cities to take the lead in forging international connections. In a world where cities increasingly become hubs of innovation, culture, and diversity, they emerge as pivotal players in shaping the global landscape. By embracing cultural diplomacy, cities can foster collaborations that transcend national boundaries, extending equality to the local level and transcending the limitations of geopolitical power dynamics.

Equality among nations finds its foothold in this holistic conception of cultural diplomacy. The power dynamics that have historically underpinned international relations are challenged, as cultural diplomacy promotes mutual respect and the recognition of every nation's unique contributions to the global narrative. The journey towards equality begins with the recognition that every nation, regardless of its size, holds a valuable piece of humanity's mosaic.

Cultural diplomacy emerges as a potent force that navigates the complex intersection of culture, diplomacy, and equality. It's a bridge connecting nations not only on a governmental level but also at the grassroots level, where civil society and cities play pivotal roles. By embracing cultural diplomacy, we embark on a journey towards harmonious international relations, where mutual understanding and respect guide our interactions. As we unravel the multidimensional facets of cultural diplomacy, we discover a path that leads to the realization of equality among nations—a path where diversity is celebrated, power dynamics are redefined, and the symphony of shared humanity resonates across borders.

GLOBAL CITIZENSHIP: THE POWER OF SHARED CULTURAL EXPERIENCES

The shared human experience lies at the heart of global citizenship. It recognizes and celebrates that we are all present together, regardless of where we are from or reside. In the end, our success and well-being are interconnected. Instead of worrying about the future, we have more to learn from one another. This profound understanding forms the crux of global citizenship—a concept that holds immense potential to foster love, peace, and, ultimately, equality among nations across the globe.

The world is undergoing an unprecedented transformation where the boundaries of identity are evolving, becoming less tethered to specific locations. This shift has profound implications for various spheres, including business, government, and society. As multinational corporations, climate change, and social and political movements continue to shape our world, the fate of humanity is undeniably interwoven.

However, amidst debates about globalization and its consequences, the essence of global citizenship often remains overshadowed. It is imperative to recalibrate our focus and recognize the pivotal role that global citizenship plays in shaping our shared future.

At its core, global citizenship comprises two dimensions: that of individuals who embrace a set of shared values and responsibilities and that of corporations that have, in the pursuit of globalization, sometimes lost sight of their role as global citizens. This distinction underscores the need for individuals and corporations to embrace global citizenship principles actively, thus paving the way for a world characterized by love, peace, and equality.

Global citizenship fundamentally revolves around the notion of the shared human experience. It celebrates the reality that we are on this journey together, irrespective of our origins or current locations. Our destinies are intrinsically intertwined, encouraging us to learn from one another rather than succumb to fear of the unknown. This essence of global citizenship is grounded in the belief that diversity enriches our collective narrative and that our interactions have the power to transcend divisions and promote understanding.

Shared principles and obligations constitute the foundation of global citizenship. Individuals who identify as global citizens recognize the profound interplay between worldwide happenings and local circumstances. They ardently support universal human rights that transcend national borders and identities, advocating for social agreements that promote equality for all. Diversity, interdependence, empathy, and perspective are central to the essence of global citizenship, empowering individuals and entities to make positive contributions across different spheres—locally, nationally, and internationally—while safeguarding the well-being of all communities.

Global citizens come from all walks of life: individuals, corporations, global nomads, and those who blend local and global identities. They span generations, gender, economic sectors, and ideologies, all united by a shared commitment to foster international understanding, love, and peace. This collective effort is underpinned by visionary leadership, where individual leaders embody shared values and corporate entities engage in governance, ethics, and investment strategies that create lasting value in the places they touch.

It's important to note that global citizenship diverges from the concept of globalization. While globalization primarily revolves around economic and business-driven influences, global citizenship is rooted in identity and shared values. Regardless of their individual roles, global citizens serve as bridge builders, risk mitigators, and guardians of our common humanity. In an era where debates about globalization can sometimes evoke tension, the role of global citizens becomes even more pivotal in maintaining harmony and promoting love and peace.

What is the significance of global citizenship?

The significance of global citizenship transcends mere existence—it holds the key to fostering love, peace, and equality among nations. Unlike innate qualities, global citizens are nurtured through education and the cultivation of global perspectives. As the world evolves, the need for global citizenship becomes increasingly imperative in shaping an environment where every nation enjoys equal rights without marginalizing the less privileged.

Historically, the roots of global citizenship were grounded in the shared aspiration to prevent conflict and war. The logic was simple: a deeper understanding of one another would breed an environment of peace, progress, and collective prosperity. More recently, groundbreaking scientific endeavors like the Human Genome Project have illuminated our shared biological origins, underscoring that we are all one. The rapid advancement of technology further enables unprecedented connectivity, allowing us to forge connections, comprehend our commonalities, navigate interdependencies, and expand our worldviews.

However, not all individuals have had the opportunity to embrace this worldview. Across the globe, countless people lack a sense of belonging. They grapple with no profound connections to other places, cultures, and fellow humans. Even within their borders, some individuals feel estranged. Particularly in developing nations, those excluded from the digital revolution find themselves on the sidelines of these transformative conversations, unveiling an uneven distribution of connectedness.

In the corporate landscape, a disheartening pattern has emerged in recent decades, with some companies prioritizing corporate interests over those of individuals, communities, and the environment. Reports of unethical conduct, corruption, exploitative labor practices, environmental degradation, and other transgressions mar the corporate world, starkly contradicting the world's needs.

Enter global citizenship—a concept that serves as a bridge to mend these divides and rectify these stark realities. Global citizens embody the essence of global citizenship and stand as the ambassadors of this transformation. Beyond a mere mindset, global citizenship propels individuals toward meaningful actions and lifestyles that nurture connections over time.

The power of global citizenship is most evident in its potential to pave the way for love, peace, and equality among nations. By embracing the principles of global citizenship, nations transcend their differences and forge bonds that unite rather than divide. Through education that encourages global perspectives, individuals learn the art of empathetic understanding, creating a ripple effect of mutual respect and cooperation that transcends borders.

Furthermore, global citizenship inherently seeks to rectify the existing disparities between nations. It addresses the imbalance that arises from the exclusion of less privileged nations from the digital revolution, striving to create an inclusive platform where every voice is heard and every perspective matters. It aims to dissolve the sense of detachment that many individuals experience at home and in relation to the broader global community.

In the corporate arena, global citizenship serves as a moral compass that redirects companies toward ethical conduct, community engagement, and environmental stewardship. By embracing a global citizenship ethos, corporations prioritize the well-being of individuals and communities over short-term profit, forging partnerships that uplift societies and protect the planet.

The concept of global citizenship stands as a testament to the power of shared cultural experiences. It is a unifying force that transcends borders and unites humanity by acknowledging our interconnectedness. By embracing global citizenship and nurturing shared values, we embark on a journey toward a world where love, peace, and equality flourish among nations. In this journey, the threads of cultural understanding intertwine to weave a tapestry of unity that bridges divides and fosters a global community rooted in mutual respect and collaboration.

PROMOTING CULTURAL EXCHANGE FOR ENHANCED GLOBAL SOLIDARITY

The perception of a harmonious world, where individuals and societies truly coexist, is a promising and challenging vision. This vision is underscored by the harsh realities of exclusion endured by millions of marginalized individuals—women, youth, migrants, and disenfranchised minorities—whose voices are often unheard amidst the cacophony of progress. Despite the surge in information, technology, and knowledge, the essence of wisdom remains indispensable in preventing conflicts, eradicating poverty, and cultivating an environment where every individual learns and lives in harmony, contributing to a safe world for all.

Amid this turbulent landscape of international globalization, a resounding message must be heralded: peace transcends the absence of warfare; it signifies a coexistence that thrives on embracing our diversity of sex, race, language, religion, and culture. A cornerstone of this coexistence is universal respect for justice and human rights, pivotal aspects underpinning the fabric of peaceful societies. It's a reminder that peace should never be taken for granted—it's a dynamic process. This enduring goal necessitates ceaseless effort, vigilance, and active participation from all corners of society. Peace isn't just a theoretical ideal; it's a conscious choice that manifests in our daily interactions, a commitment to engage in sincere dialogues with individuals and communities, whether they dwell a block away or are connected through a mere click.

In this context, the role of promoting cultural exchange emerges as a catalyst for enhanced global solidarity, a beacon guiding humanity toward love, peace, and equality among nations. Cultural exchange is more than just an exchange of artifacts or artistic expressions; it's an exchange of perspectives, stories, and ideas. It's a powerful means to transcend biases, dispel misunderstandings, and foster mutual respect, laying the foundation for a more harmonious world.

The UNESCO Universal Declaration on Cultural Diversity champions these ideals, emphasizing the importance of harmonious interaction among diverse cultural identities. It acknowledges that social cohesion, civil society vitality, and peace are nurtured by policies promoting the inclusion and participation of all citizens. Such cultural pluralism, deeply intertwined with democratic principles, nurtures cultural exchange, nurtures the flourishing of creative capacities, and fosters a public sphere where diverse voices coalesce in a symphony of unity.

For a vision of world peace to materialize, investments in education, enlightened leadership, powerful values, innovative social research, and progressive media are imperative. These elements together form the bedrock of global solidarity and are precisely the arenas in which UNESCO's mission thrives. UNESCO's enduring commitment to education and sciences, its preservation of cultural heritage and encouragement of creativity, and its pursuit of a media landscape oriented toward peace collectively contribute to the very essence of world peace—active, flourishing, and sustainable.

Through promoting cultural exchange, the path toward a peaceful world gains clarity. Cultural exchange enriches perspectives, fosters empathy, and sparks conversations beyond borders. It's a mechanism that dismantles the barriers of ignorance and prejudice, nurturing an environment where understanding thrives, and differences are celebrated. Cultural exchange empowers individuals to step beyond their comfort zones, embrace the unfamiliar with an open heart and build bridges of connection that foster international unity.

By creating platforms that facilitate cultural exchange, we create spaces for shared experiences, fostering bonds between diverse communities. These bonds, forged through dialogue and mutual understanding, establish a collective commitment to peace and equality. Cultural exchange nurtures an environment where individuals and societies engage in active learning, eradicating stereotypes, cultivating empathy, and embracing the shared values that unite humanity.

In this interconnected world, where distance is no longer defined solely by geographical boundaries, the idea of cultural exchange reverberates as a unifying force. It's a catalyst that instills a sense of common humanity, a reminder that no matter our origins, we share this planet. By actively engaging in cultural exchange, we transcend the barriers that hinder peace, equality, and coexistence among nations. We open doors to profound connections, bridge gaps in understanding, and lay the groundwork for a world where every individual's rights are upheld and the equality of nations is woven into the fabric of our global society.

CHAPTER NINE

ENSURING JUSTICE AND ACCOUNTABILITY

The threads of justice and accountability are remarkably resiliently braided. These two pillars are the cornerstones of moral governance and effective tools for maintaining international equality. Establishing strong justice and a firm commitment to accountability are essential steps toward a world where nations live in peace, harmony, and shared prosperity.

Justice is the bedrock upon which societies are built, fostering an environment where fairness, equity, and the rule of law flourish. Its significance transcends borders, extending its influence on international relations. When justice is upheld, nations are empowered to operate equitably, irrespective of their size, economic strength, or political clout. It ensures that each nation's rights are acknowledged and protected, safeguarding the very essence of equality.

Accompanying justice, accountability is a powerful compass, guiding nations towards responsible governance and transparency. It's a beacon that demands leaders and institutions to answer for their actions, policies, and decisions. In international relations, accountability compels nations to uphold their commitments, respect agreements, and adhere to the principles that underpin global stability. When nations are held accountable, the path toward equality is illuminated by a sense of trust and cooperation.

The convergence of justice and accountability on the global stage forms an intricate dance that can bolster the foundation of equality among nations. Their symbiotic relationship resonates with pursuing a world where diplomatic interactions are characterized by integrity, treaties are upheld without prejudice, and the shared goal of peaceful coexistence is fortified. As we delve deeper into justice and accountability, we uncover how these twin pillars can shape a future of harmonious international relations and sustainable equality among nations.

UPHOLDING ACCOUNTABILITY IN INTERNATIONAL RELATIONS

In the quest for more legitimacy, the call for greater accountability resounds like a light of transformation. The interaction between accountability and legitimacy has become crucial as globalization increases global connectivity and transnational entities become increasingly prominent. This intertwining of accountability and legitimacy with the overarching idea of nation-to-nation equality paints a vivid picture of how sustaining accountability can support a peaceful international environment where each nation's rights are upheld, and nation-to-nation equality thrives.

The nexus between accountability and legitimacy is a dynamic landscape, contours shaped by global governance's evolving nature. While numerous transnational actors wield substantial power and influence, the question of their legitimacy often lingers, rooted in their lack of democratic accountability. This paradox of accountability versus legitimacy presents a formidable challenge at the heart of contemporary international relations.

However, a groundbreaking shift is underway—a transformation that redefines the boundaries of accountability and charts a course toward greater legitimacy for transnational actors and international relations. Recent innovations in theoretical and practical frameworks illuminate the path where accountability, particularly when aligned with democratic standards, emerges as the linchpin for legitimizing transnational actors. This metamorphosis does not necessitate the wholesale replication of democratic mechanisms across the globe but rather harnesses the principles of accountability to breathe life into the notion of Equality of Nations.

At its core, the demand for accountability in international relations resonates as a call for authenticity—a clarion call for transnational actors to stand before the mirror of accountability and reflect their actions and decisions through the prism of democratic values. The intertwining of accountability and legitimacy is not a mere intellectual exercise; it is an inherent aspiration for a world where power is accompanied by responsibility and nations' interests, regardless of their size or stature, are safeguarded.

Accountability presents a mosaic of complexities and nuances when superimposed onto the tapestry of international relations. The pillars of accountability stand as sentinels, guardians of integrity, and guarantors of ethical conduct in a realm often fraught with power dynamics and diplomatic intricacies. This embodiment of accountability extends beyond mere transparency; it is an invitation to embrace ethical comportment, principled actions, and an unwavering commitment to honouring obligations, treaties, and agreements.

As the global stage expands to accommodate an array of actors, from nation-states to non-governmental organizations, multinational corporations, and international institutions, the call for accountability reverberates with a renewed urgency. Accountability is not confined to hierarchical relationships between states; it transcends borders and genres, permeating every interaction, negotiation, and engagement that shapes the contours of international relations.

In parallel, the march toward legitimacy takes centre stage and charts a course toward acceptance, trust, and recognition. Legitimacy is not granted through mere assertion; it is earned through a nexus of credibility, respect, and adherence to democratic values. The convergence of accountability and legitimacy in international relations is a harmonious duet, each note resonating with the aspiration for an equitable global order where nations, regardless of their economic, political, or social stature, stand on equal ground.

Within this nexus of accountability and legitimacy, the seeds of equality among nations find fertile ground. The essence of international relations—dialogue, cooperation, diplomacy—attains a new dimension when anchored in democratic values and principles of accountability. In this landscape, regardless of size or geopolitical influence, every nation can voice its concerns, contribute its perspectives, and shape humanity's collective destiny.

The marriage of accountability and legitimacy generates transformation across international relations. It transcends the boundaries of rhetoric and calls for concrete action—a recalibration of policies, practices, and governance structures to align with democratic standards. The confluence of accountability and legitimacy is not a mirage but a tangible vision of a world where nations collaborate not out of obligation but out of a shared commitment to upholding the ideals of democracy, fairness, and justice.

In this pursuit, it is essential to recognize that accountability is not a one-size-fits-all concept. The nuances of cultural contexts, historical trajectories, and governance systems all play a role in shaping the manifestation of accountability. Therefore, while the overarching principles of democratic accountability may serve as guiding stars, the pathways to achieving them must be diverse, accommodating the unique attributes of each nation.

Within this paradigm, accountability transcends being a checkmark on a list; it becomes a catalyst for nurturing trust, forging partnerships, and a new narrative of international relations—one rooted in equality and respect. The amplification of accountability doesn't fragment the global landscape; rather, it unites nations in a shared commitment to integrity, transparency, and collective well-being.

The fusion of accountability and legitimacy holds the potential to reshape the contours of international relations, carving a path toward equality among nations. This transformative journey doesn't demand the uniform replication of democratic systems worldwide; rather, it beckons the adoption of democratic values and principles of accountability as the bedrock of global interactions. As transnational actors, whether states, corporations, or organizations, embrace accountability, they sow the seeds of legitimacy and cultivate an environment where the Equality of Nations thrives. The world is on the cusp of a new era in this harmony of accountability and legitimacy. In this realm, the rights of every nation are upheld, where ethical compasses guide diplomatic interactions, and where the spirit of collaboration rests on democratic foundations.

ADDRESSING INJUSTICES THROUGH INTERNATIONAL LEGAL FRAMEWORKS

The quest for justice remains paramount in a world marked by diverse cultures, histories, and socioeconomic disparities. Injustices perpetrated by powerful nations against less powerful ones have been a recurring theme throughout history, often leading to grave human rights violations, territorial disputes, and armed conflicts. However, the evolution of international legal frameworks has provided a glimmer of hope for countering these injustices and promoting equal rights for all.

The foundation of international legal frameworks represents a pivotal paradigm shift in pursuing justice on the global stage. At its core, this foundation rests upon the profound principle of equality among nations, transcending disparities in size, power, and influence. This principle, woven intricately into the fabric of international law, is not just a lofty ideal but a transformative force that can reshape the world's dynamics.

This principle finds its resounding articulation in the Charter of the United Nations, an epoch-defining document that crystallizes the aspirations of nations to coexist in harmony while upholding justice. The Charter is a beacon of hope within its text, outlining the imperative to nurture international peace and security. It isn't merely a proclamation of intent; it underscores a commitment to prevent the scourge of conflict and the unchecked exploitation of power that has marred history.

The Charter's preamble, akin to the opening act of a grand symphony, reverberates with a declaration of faith in fundamental human rights, human dignity, and the intrinsic worth of every individual. This is no mere rhetorical flourish; it lays the groundwork for what the international legal order should embody. By anchoring itself in the value of human dignity, the Charter essentially contends that the rights and privileges of nations, regardless of their standing, must be safeguarded.

Moreover, the Charter's invocation of cooperation calls to transcend the parochial confines of nationalism and egoism. It echoes the idea that nations can mitigate disparities and foster a sense of mutual responsibility by working collectively. Injustice often thrives in the vacuum of isolation; cooperation, on the other hand, bolsters the edifice of justice, rendering it resilient and universally applicable.

The Charter's proclamation is not confined to diplomatic rhetoric; it is a rallying cry for establishing a just world order. A community where the historical power imbalances that have given rise to injustices are tackled through ethical contemplation and legal boundaries. This path leads to a society where those in positions of power are answerable, where the marginalized and vulnerable are shielded, and where the fundamental principles of human rights remain beyond challenge.

In essence, the Charter is a living testament to the notion that the collective consciousness of nations can evolve. It signifies the dawning of an era where international legal frameworks are not just instruments of regulation but of transformation. It encourages the belief that equality among nations is not an unattainable ideal but a tangible reality that can be woven into the tapestry of global interactions.

As we navigate the complex geopolitical terrain of the modern world, the foundational principle enshrined within the Charter continues to be a lodestar. It propels us towards a horizon where the rule of law prevails over the rule of might, where justice isn't confined to the fortunate few but extends its protective embrace to all corners of the world. In embracing this principle, humanity takes a bold step toward a just and equitable future, where international legal frameworks are guardians of a world order that cherishes the inherent worth of every nation.

Learning from Past Injustices

History serves as an invaluable teacher, offering profound insights into the consequences of unchecked power and the imperative of addressing past injustices. The annals of time abound with examples of powerful nations wielding their advantages to subjugate weaker counterparts, resulting in a legacy of suffering and subverted sovereignty. The spectra of colonialism, imperialism, and annexation loom large over societies across continents, bearing witness to the enduring scars of exploitation.

World War II, a cataclysmic confluence of humanity's darkest impulses, is a pivotal juncture that thrust the world into the reckoning. With its atrocities and mass-scale injustices, the horrors of that conflict laid bare the depths to which power could descend when unbridled by ethical restraint. However, amidst the rubble and ruin emerged a newfound resolve within the international community to prevent such catastrophes from recurring.

The crucible of World War II birthed initiatives that sought to channel humanity's collective trauma into transformative action. The Nuremberg Trials, a landmark legal endeavor, exemplified the commitment to dismantling the architecture of impunity that had shielded those responsible for egregious crimes. The creation of the International Military Tribunal marked a pivotal departure from traditional notions of sovereign immunity, as it embarked on a journey to prosecute individuals irrespective of their nationality or status.

These trials, more than delivering retribution, sowed the seeds of accountability. By subjecting even the most powerful to the scrutiny of justice, they underscored that the mantle of power doesn't confer immunity to perpetuate injustice. This marked a seismic shift in international law, encapsulating the spirit of "never again." The scars of past injustices etched deep into the collective memory, fueled the evolution of a legal framework that would aspire to transcend power imbalances and preserve the sanctity of human rights.

Essentially, history's lessons are etched into the fabric of international legal frameworks. The wounds inflicted by colonial oppression and genocidal horrors sparked a profound change in collective global awareness. As a result, institutions emerged, poised to guard against upcoming injustices. The significance of the Nuremberg Trials and the formation of the International Military Tribunal extended beyond mere symbols; they stood as proof of humanity's unwavering resolve to confront its darker aspects and carve a route toward a fairer world.

The Power of International Courts and Tribunals

The power of international courts and tribunals is a testament to the collective commitment of nations to ensure that justice transcends borders and might is tempered by accountability. At the heart of addressing global injustices lies the establishment of these judicial entities, which play a crucial role in navigating complex international disputes and upholding the principles of fairness and equity.

The International Court of Justice (ICJ), affectionately known as the "World Court," stands as a beacon of hope in this endeavor. As the primary legal entity within the United Nations, the ICJ can settle conflicts between nations and provide expert legal advice on complex matters when referred by UN bodies. Its existence is not merely ceremonial; it's a testament to the evolution of international law and the recognition that even the mightiest nations should be subject to legal scrutiny.

The ICJ's pivotal role becomes evident when examining landmark cases that have shaped its jurisprudence. In the case of Nicaragua v. United States, the ICJ asserted its authority by ruling against the United States for its actions in Nicaragua, highlighting that even powerful nations cannot act with impunity. Similarly, the Bosnia and Herzegovina v. Serbia case showcased the ICJ's commitment to holding states accountable for their actions during conflict and ensuring that justice prevails over political considerations.

These cases signify a departure from an era when power imbalances often dictated the outcome of international disputes. The ICJ transcends the limitations of power politics by virtue of its impartiality and adherence to the rule of law. Its decisions are legally binding and serve as a moral compass pointing towards a world where national boundaries do not confine justice.

However, the power of international courts and tribunals goes beyond individual cases. They create a precedent that reshapes the landscape of international relations. The mere knowledge that actions can be brought before a court of international law encourages restraint and discourages nations from trampling upon the rights and sovereignty of others. This, in turn, fosters a culture of accountability and cooperation, underscoring that the pursuit of justice is a shared responsibility.

International courts and tribunals are the threads that weave together the principles of equality, fairness, and accountability. They stand as symbols of the potential for justice to transcend geopolitical divides and ensure that the rights and dignity of nations, irrespective of their power, are upheld. As we grapple with the complexities of a globalized world, these institutions illuminate a path toward a future where borders or circumstances do not confine the pursuit of justice. Still, they are an indomitable force that shapes the fabric of international relations.

Promotion of Human Rights and Humanitarian Law

Promoting human rights and humanitarian law represents a fundamental pillar in the edifice of international legal frameworks. These guiding principles, rooted in profound reverence for human dignity, stand as a bulwark against the capricious exercise of power and serve as a rallying cry for justice in the face of adversity.

The Universal Declaration of Human Rights, a monumental accomplishment of 1948, emphatically proclaims the fundamental rights of each individual. This extraordinary document, conceived in reaction to the horrors of World War II, transcends boundaries of culture, nationality, and ideology. It is a blueprint for protecting universal and indivisible rights, recognizing that the sanctity of human dignity is the foundation upon which just societies are built.

Central to the Universal Declaration is the notion that governments do not bestow rights but are inherent to every human being. This acknowledgement fundamentally alters power dynamics by emphasizing that even the mightiest nations are bound to respect and uphold these rights. From the right to life and liberty to the right to education and cultural participation, the declaration outlines a comprehensive tapestry of human rights that transcend the vagaries of circumstance.

Furthermore, the Geneva Conventions and their Additional Protocols underscore the urgency of protecting human rights even during armed conflict. These conventions, distilled from the crucible of the horrors of war, offer a framework that seeks to minimize the suffering inflicted on civilians, prisoners of war, and the wounded. By establishing rules that govern the treatment of those ensnared in the maelstrom of conflict, these conventions exemplify a commitment to preserving human dignity even in the darkest hours.

Promoting human rights and humanitarian law is an unwavering declaration that power is subject to ethical restraint. It is a countermeasure against the arrogance of might, ensuring that the strong are held accountable for their actions and the vulnerable are shielded from the excesses of unchecked power. These principles transcend cultural differences, reminding us that preserving human dignity is a shared endeavour transcending borders and histories.

Promoting human rights and humanitarian law isn't merely a legalistic exercise; it's a profound statement of our collective commitment to humanity. This declaration underscores the idea that our collective principles hold more power than the conflicts attempting to divide us and that steadfast dedication to justice is imperative, irrespective of the situations at hand. In embracing these principles, we affirm our shared humanity and take a step closer to a world where the rights of all individuals are inviolable and the pursuit of justice is an unassailable force.

Fact-Driven Advocacy

Propelled by meticulously gathered data, fact-driven advocacy is a formidable weapon against injustice. In an era where information is an indispensable currency of influence, organizations like Amnesty International and Human Rights Watch play a pivotal role in unveiling the truths that might otherwise remain obscured in the shadows of power.

Armed with a commitment to justice and a relentless pursuit of truth, these organizations engage in a meticulous documentation process. Their reports are not mere narratives but meticulously constructed narratives that rely on a constellation of evidence. From satellite imagery that captures the footprint of destruction to eyewitness accounts that witness atrocities, data collation is a tapestry woven from diverse sources, each thread adding depth to the narrative of injustice.

The power of fact-driven advocacy lies in its ability to shatter the illusion of deniability. Data transcends rhetoric; it presents a tangible, irrefutable account of events. When satellite images reveal the obliteration of villages, forensic evidence discloses the scars of torture, and eyewitnesses courageously testify to their experiences. The result is an indisputable narrative that demands attention.

These meticulously constructed reports serve as a mirror that reflects the face of injustice back to the world. They provide a voice to the voiceless and galvanize global consciousness. The power of data-driven advocacy becomes even more pronounced when it is wielded against powerful nations. In the face of documented evidence, political considerations find themselves at odds with a groundswell of public awareness and international pressure.

The credibility of these organizations hinges on the rigor of their methodology. The transparency with which they gather, verify, and present data lends weight to their findings. The impartiality of their efforts serves as a counterbalance to the vested interests that often cloud the pursuit of justice.

In an increasingly interconnected world, fact-driven advocacy is not just a conduit for change but a catalyst. It transforms abstract notions of injustice into concrete realities, demanding accountability and redress. As these organizations navigate the complex terrain of power dynamics, their reliance on accurate data declares that the pursuit of justice is not confined to lofty ideals—it is a tangible endeavor fueled by evidence that challenges the powerful to confront the consequences of their actions.

In the ongoing struggle against injustice, fact-driven advocacy is a beacon of hope. It reinforces the understanding that truth is a force to be reckoned with, capable of piercing through the veils of secrecy and impunity. By wielding data as a sword and transparency as a shield, these organizations remind us that even in the face of the mightiest challenges, the pursuit of justice remains an indomitable force, fueled by facts and illuminated by the unwavering commitment of those who seek a more just world.

The Role of Diplomacy and Multilateralism

The role of diplomacy and multilateralism in addressing injustices is akin to the conductor's baton guiding an intricate symphony of global relations. In a world where power imbalances and divergent interests often collide, diplomacy is the art of bridging divides, preventing conflicts, and fostering cooperation. Multilateral organizations, exemplified by the United Nations (UN), stand as essential arenas for these diplomatic endeavors.

Diplomacy is not just the sterile exchange of words; it's the arena where conflicts are defused, negotiations chart the path toward compromise, and dialogue replaces confrontation. Multilateral platforms like the UN provide a stage where nations can engage in discourse, seeking common ground and resolutions to conflicts. These diplomatic engagements, often conducted behind closed doors, hold the potential to redirect the trajectory of events, preventing escalations that could lead to injustice.

Furthermore, the multilateral approach encompasses more than dialogue—it encompasses action. Peacekeeping missions, for instance, exemplify the international community's commitment to prevent injustices from escalating into full-fledged conflicts. These missions, deploying troops to conflict zones, act as a buffer, safeguarding civilians and upholding the principles of humanitarian law.

Diplomacy's reach extends even to situations where injustice has already occurred. Mediation efforts, facilitated by impartial third parties, aim to repair the ruptured fabric of societies torn apart by strife. These efforts seek not just to end violence but address the root causes of injustice, paving the way for sustainable peace and reconciliation.

Another facet of diplomacy, sanctions regimes wield economic and political pressure to dissuade nations from perpetuating injustices. While controversial, sanctions can serve as a non-violent mechanism to curb the excesses of power and compel nations to reconsider their actions.

The Rome Statute's formation of the International Criminal Court (ICC) marks the highest point in cooperative efforts to abolish impunity. The ICC promotes a culture of accountability by prosecuting people for the most severe international crimes and highlighting that no one is above the law.

This mechanism serves as a deterrent against future wrongdoings by reinforcing to wrongdoers that their deeds will not escape consequences.

In essence, diplomacy and multilateralism form a dynamic duo in pursuing justice. They are conduits through which nations, regardless of their power, engage in meaningful dialogue, prevent conflicts, and foster accountability. These mechanisms emphasize that a shared commitment to justice is the cornerstone of global stability. As we navigate the intricate labyrinth of international relations, diplomacy and multilateralism remind us that the pursuit of justice is not just an individual endeavour; it's a collaborative symphony that resonates with the aspirations of all nations for a more just and equitable world.

Successes and Challenges

Significant successes and enduring challenges mark the journey to address injustices through international legal frameworks. These complexities underscore the intricate nature of global power dynamics and the intricacies of justice on a global scale.

International legal frameworks, emphasizing equality and accountability have achieved remarkable milestones. Establishing international courts, developing human rights conventions, and creating mechanisms like the ICC have collectively fostered a culture of accountability and deterrence against impunity. Landmark cases and successful prosecutions have demonstrated that justice can transcend borders and power imbalances.

However, challenges persist, often rooted in the asymmetrical power distribution and competing national interests. One notable challenge is the selective enforcement of international law, where powerful nations might evade accountability for their actions due to their geopolitical influence. This can undermine the credibility of the legal frameworks and erode public trust in their efficacy.

Reluctance by powerful nations to subject themselves to legal scrutiny can be another obstacle. Some nations might view their sovereignty as a shield against international legal mechanisms, leading to a need for more cooperation in investigations and trials. This challenges the principle of equal accountability before the law, and the absence of consequences can perpetuate injustices.

Geopolitical considerations further complicate the pursuit of justice. The intricacies of international relations often lead to compromises and diplomatic maneuvering that can dilute the impact of legal frameworks. This can be particularly detrimental in cases where justice is sacrificed for the sake of political expediency.

The United States withdrawal from the ICC and its hesitation to ratify key human rights treaties exemplify these challenges. While the United States has cited concerns over the potential politicization of legal processes, these actions also highlight the tensions between powerful nations and international legal institutions.

While international legal frameworks have made commendable progress in combating injustices, the path is fraught with challenges that stem from power dynamics and political considerations. Overcoming these challenges requires a collective commitment from nations, a reiteration of the principles enshrined in these frameworks, and a shared understanding that justice cannot be compromised for expediency. As the world grapples with these complexities, the successes achieved so far stand as beacons of hope, guiding the way toward a more just and equitable global order.

International legal frameworks provide a roadmap for change in a world still grappling with the scars of historical injustices and contemporary power dynamics. Through a combination of legal mechanisms, fact-driven advocacy, diplomacy, and multilateralism, these frameworks stand as a formidable arsenal against injustice. The evolution of international law reflects humanity's collective commitment to ensuring equal rights for all, regardless of their place on the global stage. Embracing the principles of accountability, cooperation, and justice will be paramount in building a world where power is not a license to oppress but a responsibility to uphold the dignity of all nations.

TRUTH AND RECONCILIATION: NAVIGATING THE PATH TO GLOBAL JUSTICE

Throughout history, stories of grief, suffering, and injustice have reverberated through generations, leaving wounds on the collective psyche of nations. The urgent appeal for justice, truth, and healing reverberates in the quest for a peaceful global environment. Against this backdrop, the Global Initiative for Justice, Truth, and Reconciliation emerges—a coalition of nine global organizations that serve as beacons of hope, guiding communities toward a future built on healing, understanding, and equity.

In the face of human rights crimes, the Global Initiative for Justice, Truth, and Reconciliation has transformed and is a living example of the strength of group action.

This consortium of global organizations serves as a conduit through which the voices of survivors rise above the cacophony of pain, finding resonance in the corridors of power and the hearts of individuals worldwide. As it works alongside communities, this initiative doesn't just address the shadows of the past; it crafts a narrative that shapes the contours of the future.

The essence of this endeavor lies in its recognition that by addressing past trauma, we have the power to shape a future free from the shackles of injustice. The journey of truth and reconciliation is not just a movement but a paradigm shift—a profound transformation that navigates the delicate intricacies of healing, acknowledgement, and empowerment.

The Journey of Truth

At the heart of the truth and reconciliation process lies a profound journey—an expedition into the depths of history to unveil hidden narratives, casting a light on the shadows that have shaped our world. This journey isn't merely an academic exercise; it's a transformative odyssey that signifies the triumph of humanity's collective commitment to confront past injustices and heal the wounds that continue to fester.

Truth, in the context of reconciliation, becomes more than a historical record; it becomes a beacon of hope, a clarion call to reckon with the unvarnished realities relegated to the fringes of our consciousness. The process transcends recounting events; it's about laying bare the fabric of human experience—the pain, the suffering, and the courage that defines it.

Unveiling hidden narratives is an act of immense courage. It's about giving voice to those who have been silenced, those whose stories have been buried beneath layers of denial and indifference. The truth-telling process magnifies the voices of survivors, honoring their resilience and transforming them into agents of change. In sharing their stories, survivors transcend victimhood, becoming torchbearers of a brighter future.

Truth-telling is not confined to the past; it has profound implications for the present and future. By bringing the truth to light, nations and communities lay the groundwork for understanding and empathy. It's a catalyst for breaking down the barriers that have divided societies, cultivating a culture of openness, and fostering a shared commitment to justice.

Moreover, truth-telling is instrumental in planting the seeds of accountability. As the hidden narratives are brought to the forefront, they become impossible to ignore. Denial dissipates, and the clamor for justice gains momentum. Individuals and institutions responsible for past injustices are confronted with the weight of their actions, and the pursuit of accountability becomes imperative for a just society.

However, the journey of truth is not without its challenges. It requires confronting uncomfortable truths and navigating the complexities of memory and perception. But it is through these challenges that the journey gains its transformative power. As wounds are cleaned up and addressed rather than left to fester, society may start the process of healing and reconciliation via these difficult conversations.

The journey of truth represents the dawning of a new chapter in the story of humanity—a chapter characterized by honesty, compassion, and a shared commitment to justice. It's a journey that unveils hidden narratives, not to perpetuate pain but to pave a path toward healing. It's a reminder that the pursuit of truth is a testament to our collective resilience and the understanding that we can only shape a more equitable and harmonious future by acknowledging the past.

The Power of Reconciliation

While the truth lays bare the wounds of history, reconciliation emerges as a potent force, a bridge that spans, divides and leads toward the intricate path of healing. Reconciliation is not a mere act of forgetting or sidestepping the past; it's a courageous act of acknowledging pain, embracing vulnerability, and weaving bonds that transcend the scars of history.

After the truth-telling process has begun to mend the fabric of understanding, reconciliation becomes the canvas upon which nations and communities paint their shared aspirations. This journey, though complex, is essential in constructing a cohesive future. Reconciliation is about more than just closing the chapter on past grievances; it's about fostering connections that are stronger than historical wounds and a commitment to building a more harmonious world.

The process of reconciliation demands a delicate balance. It requires acknowledging the injustices that have transpired, honoring the pain of those who have suffered, and facing the discomfort of historical realities head-on. At the same time, it beckons nations and individuals to step beyond the boundaries of history, recognizing that the pursuit of an equitable future is the common ground they share.

Gestures of empathy and acts of restitution are key ingredients of reconciliation. Apologies and reparations can serve as bridges, facilitating the journey toward healing. Through these acts, a shared commitment to justice and a desire for equity are palpably communicated. Reconciliation isn't about wiping the slate clean; it's about acknowledging and confronting history with courage and resilience.

Ultimately, the essence of reconciliation resides in the sincere aspiration to build a society where each individual's rights are recognized and celebrated. It's about upholding the principles of justice and ensuring that no one is left behind in the march toward progress.

In global justice, reconciliation connects countries and communities, bridging gaps in the past and forming a strong foundation for the future. It is evidence of the capacity of humanity to convert suffering into comprehension, wounds into knowledge, and divisions into connections. By accepting reconciliation, the world takes a step toward a future in which equity rules and the scars of the past are turned into rays of hope.

Global Justice: Weaving the Equity Thread

The unfolding Global Initiative for Justice, Truth, and Reconciliation is a profound testament to the inextricable connection between justice and equity, illuminating a path toward fairness and harmony. This initiative is more than a symbolic gesture; it embodies the profound belief that the pursuit of global justice rests on the pillars of truth and reconciliation.

Global justice isn't an abstract notion; it's a tangible reality that emerges when nations and communities confront their history honestly and embrace a collective responsibility for their actions. This pursuit necessitates acknowledging past injustices, no matter how uncomfortable, and working ardently to forge a future defined by impartiality and mutual respect.

Establishing an equitable global environment isn't a passive outcome but a dynamic process that demands concerted efforts. Addressing historical wrongs requires an unflinching commitment to introspection as nations grapple with the shadows of their past. The process of truth and reconciliation serves as the crucible where these principles are forged. The pain of past transgressions becomes the impetus for positive change, where the legacy of injustice is transformed into a shared resolve to uphold justice.

This process doesn't merely seek to erase history but aims to rewrite it to foster unity, understanding, and shared values. It's a journey that necessitates acknowledging the voices of those who have suffered, providing a platform for their stories to be heard, and working together to prevent the repetition of past mistakes.

In this pursuit of global justice, truth becomes the bedrock upon which equity is built. Reconciliation isn't a passive agreement; it's an active endeavor that requires nations and communities to look each other in the eye, acknowledge their shared humanity, and commit to a future of empathy and fairness.

As the Global Initiative for Justice, Truth, and Reconciliation unfolds, it exemplifies the resilience of the human spirit and the potential for positive change. It serves as a clarion call for nations to engage in a collective endeavor to weave the fabric of equity—a fabric that is strengthened by the threads of truth and reconciliation. In embracing this initiative, the world takes a significant stride toward a future where justice isn't just a lofty ideal but a living reality that resonates with the shared aspirations of all nations.

Championing Global Equality

The journey of truth and reconciliation offers profound insights into how a truly equitable environment—one that champions the equal rights of all nations—can be established. It showcases the power of acknowledging historical wrongs and listening to the voices of survivors, recognizing their experiences as valid and essential components of our global narrative.

The Worldwide Initiative for Justice, Truth, and Reconciliation is an actual instance of the transformative power of truth and reconciliation and provides a model for worldwide equality. It illustrates that the past need not determine the present or the future, that reconciliation is possible, and that nations can move past the wounds of the past to build a world in which each country's rights are honored.

Truth and reconciliation are not abstract notions; they serve as agents of transformation that can reshape the course of our world. The Global Initiative for Justice, Truth, and Reconciliation symbolizes hope, leading nations and communities toward a future built upon the pillars of equality, justice, and mutual comprehension.

As the echoes of survivors› voices grow louder and the narrative of history is rewritten, the path to global justice becomes clearer—a path where the principles of equality among nations are upheld, and the tapestry of our world is woven with threads of truth, reconciliation, and lasting peace. This path leads us to an equitable world where nations stand united, bound by the bonds of shared humanity and the promise of equal rights for all.

CREATING A WORLD WHERE JUSTICE PREVAILS FOR ALL NATIONS

Creating a world where justice prevails for all nations is a grand endeavor that requires a multifaceted and comprehensive approach. It entails addressing past injustices and laying the foundation for a future where equity, fairness, and respect are the cornerstones of international relations. To achieve this vision, several key strategies must be employed.

1. Strengthening International Legal Frameworks:
   Strengthening and upholding international legal frameworks is crucial in building a world with equity and justice for all nations. These foundational structures, including the United Nations Charter, the Universal Declaration of Human Rights, and a range of international treaties, form the cornerstone of advancing human rights, averting conflicts, and ensuring nations are answerable for their deeds. Nations must reaffirm their commitment to these frameworks and work collaboratively to ensure effective implementation.

2. Fostering Multilateral Cooperation:
   Multilateralism is essential in promoting equity and justice on a global scale. Multilateral organizations like the United Nations provide dialogue, negotiation, and conflict resolution platforms. By fostering cooperation among nations, these organizations can address common challenges, promote understanding, and prevent the abuse of power. Collaborative efforts can lead to the formulation of equitable solutions that consider the interests of all nations.

3. Ensuring Accountability and Reconciliation:
   Accountability for past injustices is paramount in building a just world. Truth and reconciliation processes, international courts, and tribunals are critical in addressing historical wrongs. Pursuing accountability demonstrates that no nation is above the law and that justice transcends power dynamics. Acknowledging past mistakes, offering reparations, and working toward reconciliation can pave the way for healing and a more equitable future.

4. Promoting Human Rights and Dignity:
   Central to the concept of justice is promoting and protecting human rights and human dignity. Nations must commit to upholding every individual's fundamental rights, irrespective of nationality, ethnicity, or socioeconomic status. By nurturing a culture that upholds human rights, countries can establish a setting conducive to equality, reducing the likelihood of injustices.

5. Addressing Economic Disparities:
   Economic inequalities often underlie many global injustices. Tackling these imbalances demands a collaborative endeavor to bolster comprehensive economic expansion, eliminate poverty, and guarantee universal access to essentials across all nations. Embracing equitable trade practices, conscientious investments, and well-structured developmental projects can serve as tools to narrow the economic gap and advance fairness.

6. Supporting Education and Awareness:
   Education is a powerful tool in shaping a just world. By promoting education that emphasizes tolerance, cultural understanding, and empathy, nations can help combat ignorance and prejudice. Educated citizens are more likely to demand accountability, support human rights, and work toward improving society.

7. Promoting Dialogue and Conflict Resolution:
   Diplomacy and peaceful conflict resolution mechanisms are essential in preventing and addressing injustices. Nations must prioritize open and honest dialogue to bridge divides and find common ground. Mediation efforts, peacekeeping missions, and negotiation processes can prevent conflicts from escalating and promote lasting solutions.

8. Encouraging Ethical Leadership:
   Leadership assumes a pivotal role in steering the course of the world. Ethical leaders, emphasizing justice, transparency, and accountability, have the power to establish a constructive precedent for nations. Ethical leadership cultivates a milieu wherein the concerns of all nations are taken into account, and choices are formulated with the overarching welfare in perspective.

9. Empowering Civil Society and Media:
   Civil society organizations and independent media function as crucial overseers, holding nations accountable for their deeds. By empowering these entities and safeguarding their autonomy, societies can remain well-informed, demand justice, and champion transformation whenever necessary.

10. Committing to Sustainable Development:
    Sustainable development goes hand in hand with justice. Nations can build a world where equity and justice are interwoven with

environmental stewardship by ensuring that resources are managed responsibly, minimizing environmental degradation, and the present mistakes do not burden future generations.

In conclusion, building a world where justice prevails for all nations is a complex but essential aspiration. It requires the collective commitment of nations to address past injustices, promote accountability, and create an environment where equity and fairness are the norm. By strengthening international legal frameworks, fostering multilateral cooperation, promoting human rights, addressing economic disparities, and embracing ethical leadership, nations can work together to shape a brighter future. This vision necessitates a relentless dedication to truth, reconciliation, and the pursuit of a global order that respects the dignity and rights of all individuals, regardless of their nationality or background. As nations come together with a shared sense of purpose, the dream of a just and equitable world can be transformed into a reality that benefits every corner of the globe.

CONCLUSION

In this comprehensive examination of the intricate interplay between the sovereignty of nations, the imperative for a more equitable global economic framework and the role of cooperative multilateralism, this book explains how to understand the evolving dynamics of our interconnected world.

At the heart of this exploration lies the concept of sovereignty. Once a steadfast fortress guarding a nation's autonomy, this traditional understanding no longer encapsulates the complexities of our modern reality. The emergence of global challenges transcending borders—such as climate change, terrorism, and pandemics—has underscored the limitations of unilateral sovereignty. In response, we find the need to reassess this notion, recognizing that true sovereignty thrives when nations embrace cooperative action, pooling their strengths to address shared predicaments.

The question then arises: how does the recalibration of sovereignty align with the demand for a more equitable global economic architecture? The current system, dominated by unequal wealth distribution and power imbalances, perpetuates economic disparities that undermine the sovereignty of countless nations. Economic inequality is not solely an ethical concern; it impedes peaceful relations and global stability. The vision of a just economic order calls for a shift from an individualistic, profit-driven mindset to one that prioritizes the well-being of all citizens, regardless of their nation's economic stature.

Economic equality and the equal rights of nations are inextricably linked. The quest for global justice necessitates acknowledging every nation's inherent dignity and worth, regardless of size or economic clout. Just as individuals possess equal human rights, nations should share equal rights in international affairs. This principle embodies the essence of sovereignty—one that encapsulates both independence and interdependence. This transformative perspective paves the way for a world where cooperation is not perceived as a compromise of sovereignty but rather as an assertion of it.

As exemplified by multilateral agreements, cooperation serves as the bridge between these seemingly divergent concepts. The misconception that sovereignty and cooperation are mutually exclusive is debunked as we recognize that multilateral frameworks amplify nations' sovereignty rather than dilute it. Multilateralism extends beyond mere diplomatic collaboration; it embodies the collective pursuit of shared goals, where the interests of one nation intertwine with those of others. Through this lens, we understand that multilateral agreements are not external controls infringing upon sovereignty; they are instruments of enhanced sovereignty, providing a platform for nations to shape their collective destiny.

The embodiment of this principle lies in the equality of votes within international institutions. The United Nations, the World Trade Organization, and other global bodies illustrate the democratic essence of sovereignty—each nation, regardless of its economic or political stature, holds an equal vote. This principle is not a compromise but empowerment of sovereignty, for it ensures that the smallest voices resonate as loudly as the largest, creating an arena where true cooperative multilateralism can flourish.

The imperative to forge a path towards cooperative multilateralism is more than an academic exercise. It is a moral, ethical, and practical necessity. The lessons learned to underline the urgency of advocating for equality among nations in every facet of international relations. By embracing this advocacy, we perpetuate a legacy that transcends individual nations—a legacy of unity, shared prosperity, and the collective pursuit of a more just and equitable world.

The exploration through the nexus of sovereignty, economic equality, and cooperative multilateralism in this book extends an invitation to world leaders and all of humanity, encouraging us to reshape our perspectives and redefine our priorities. It urges us to shed antiquated notions and instead adopt a holistic understanding of sovereignty—one that flourishes hand in hand with cooperation. This journey challenges us to break down the barriers of economic inequality, recognizing that the pursuit of equality is an intrinsic facet of sovereignty. It empowers us to ardently advocate for multilateral agreements, recognizing them as instrumental platforms for cultivating shared sovereignty and global advancement.

This narrative is not confined to the pages of this exploration. It is a living dialogue that demands our ongoing engagement and advocacy. As the world navigates complex geopolitical shifts and faces multifaceted challenges, our uncovered principles offer a beacon of hope and a roadmap for action. We stand at a crossroads where the trajectories of nations and the destiny of humanity converge. Let us march forward, armed with the knowledge that sovereignty and cooperation are not adversaries but allies on the path towards a world that embraces the inherent dignity of all nations and fosters a legacy of equality, peace, and shared prosperity.

REFERENCES

- Ansong, A. (2016). *The concept of sovereign equality of states in international law*
- Buchs, C., & Maradan, M. (2021). Fostering equity in a multicultural and multilingual classroom through cooperative learning. *Intercultural Education.*
- Carley, S., & Konisky, D. M. (2020). The justice and equity implications of the clean energy transition. *Nature Energy,*
- Schroeder, D., Chatfield, K., Singh, M., Chennells, R., & Herissone-Kelly, P. (2019). The four values framework: fairness, respect, care and honesty. In *SpringerBriefs in research and innovation governance.*
- Lowe, V. (2015). 4. Freedom from external interference. In *Oxford University Press eBooks.*
- Krasner, S. D. (April, 2019). Think again: sovereignty. *Foreign Policy.*
- Williams, D. (n.d.). *Managing Sovereignty: The World Bank And Development in Sub-Saharan Africa.*
- Hasa. (2021). What is the Difference Between Internal and External Sovereignty in Sociology. *Pediaa.Com.*
- Hughes, A., & Hughes, A. (July, 2019). The essential nature of borders in ensuring sovereignty - constituting America. *Constituting America.*
- Bickerton, C. J., Brack, N., Coman, R., & Crespy, A. (2022). Conflicts of sovereignty in contemporary Europe: a framework of analysis. *Comparative European Politics.*

- Oyedokun, D. M. (2021). An assessment of the impact of globalisation on the sovereignty of the new states in global affairs. *ResearchGate.*
- Dorussen, H., Gartzke, E., & Westerwinter, O. (2016). Networked international politics. *Journal of Peace Research, 53*(3), 283–291.
- Smith, J. D. (2015). Geographies of interdependence. *Geography, 100*(1), 12–19.
- Kawai, M. (July, 2020). *New Global Economic Architecture: the Asian Perspective.* Asian Development Bank.
- *Top Ten Global Economic Challenges: An Assessment of Global Risks and Priorities | Brookings.* (August, 2017). Brookings.
- O'Rourke, T. W., & Iammarino, N. K. (2006). The American Mirage of Equality—Is Social Justice myth or reality? *American Journal of Health Education.*
- Times, N. Y. (December, 1934). EQUALITY: THE JAPANESE MIRAGE; *The New York Times.*
- Roe, E. (1991). Development narratives or making the best of blueprint development. *World Development.*
- Aiyar, S. (2023). Geo-Economic fragmentation and the future of multilateralism. *Imfsg.*
- Sanderson, D. (March, 2019). *How to treat First Nations as equals? Abandon your "consultations."* Policy Options.
- Lietaer, B., Arnsperger, C., Goerner, S. & Brunnhuber, S. 2012. *Money and Sustainability*: The missing link. A report from the Club of Rome – EU Chapter. Triarchy Press.
- NEF (New Economics Foundation) 2015. People Powered Money: *Designing, developing & delivering community currencies.*
- North, P. 2010. Local Money: *How to make it happen in your community.* Transition Books.
- North, P. 2007. Money and Liberation: *The micropolitics of alternative currency movements.* University of Minnesota Pres
- Nicolle, K. (2022). Responsible Resource management. *Southern African Wildlife College.*

- Iancu, A. (2020). Reserve currencies in an evolving international monetary system. *Imfsg.*
- De Zwart, P. (2019). The global history of inequality. *International Review of Social History,*
- Emmenegger, P., Häusermann, S., & Walter, S. (2018). National Sovereignty vs. International Cooperation: Policy Choices in Trade-Off Situations. *Swiss Political Science Review.*
- Stern, P. C., & Druckman, D. (2000). International conflict resolution after the Cold War. In *National Academies Press eBooks.*
- Thomas, W. (n.d.). The diplomacy of collaboration. *CDOTrends | Digital & Data Insights for Business Leaders.*
- Kaya, A. (2015). Designing the multilateral trading system: Voting equality at the International Trade Organization. *World Trade Review.*
- Luo, H., & Yang, L. (2021). Equality and equity in emerging multilateral financial institutions: the case of the BRICS institutions. *Global Policy.*
- Montero, F. J. (n.d.). :: *Multilateral Treaties > Department of International Law > OAS.*
- Bodansky, D., & Diringer, E. (2010). The Evolution of International Regimes: Implications for climate change. *Social Science Research Network.*
- Downs, George W., David M. Rocke, and Peter Barsoom. 1997. Designing Multilaterals: *The Architecture and Evolution of Environmental Agreements.*
- Harry. 1995. From EEA to EU: Economic Consequences for the EFTA Countries. European Economic Review. *Regionalization of the World Economy. Chicago: University of Chicago Press.*
- Gestrin, Michael, and Alan M. Rugman. 1994. Economic Regionalism in Latin America. *International Journal.*
- Stieb, D. M., Huang, A., Hocking, R., Crouse, D. L., Osornio-Vargas, A., & Villeneuve, P. J. (2019). Using maps to communicate

environmental exposures and health risks: Review and best-practice recommendations. *Environmental Research.*

- Ekhator, E. (2023). "Environmental Justice in the Global South: Overview of some Contemporary Developments". *Social Science Research Network.*
- Grasso, M. (2023). Climate Justice from Theory to Practice: The Responsibility and Duties of the Oil Industry. *E-International Relations.*
- Boyce, J. K. (2018). The environmental cost of inequality. *Scientific American, 319*(5), 72–77.
- Bryant, G. (2016). Creating a level playing field? The concentration and centralisation of emissions in the European Union Emissions Trading System. *Energy Policy, 99*, 308–318.
- Akilli, E. (2022). Exploring Heritage Diplomacy: The Belt and Road Initiative (BRI) Western Balkans. In *Springer eBooks.*
- Qin, Y. (2020). Diplomacy as Relational Practice. *The Hague Journal of Diplomacy.*
- Carothers, T., & Brechenmacher, S. (2014). Accountability, transparency, participation, and inclusion: a new development consensus? *Carnegie Endowment for International Peace.*
- Grover, L. (2019). Transitional Justice, international law and the United Nations. *Nordic Journal of International Law.*

About The Author:

Dr. Dominion V. Judah is a distinguished economist, visionary scientist, accomplished researcher, and prolific innovator. With an unwavering commitment to elevating lives, businesses, communities, and nations, he stands as a grand trailblazer and pathfinder in different fields, the academia and practical applications. Driven by an unyielding passion for progress, he has authored numerous bestselling books, each a testament to his relentless pursuit of knowledge and improvement, some of which include "Sub-national Prosperity," "Peace And Not War," "Economic Renaissance," "Ending Poverty", "Economics and Finance Win-Win Growth Strategies"

Dr. Dominion V. Judah epitomizes the convergence of intellectual rigor and humanitarian fervor. His profound contributions have not only enriched scholarly discourse but have also ignited tangible change in the lives of countless individuals, communities and nations. Through his visionary work, he continues to illuminate the path towards a future marked by empowered economies, poverty-free societies, world peace and lasting global transformation.